THE ILLUSTRATED GUIDE TO
PLATFORM TENNIS

THE ILLUSTRATED GUIDE TO

PLATFORM TENNIS

By Bill Ballard & Jim Hevener
of the New Jersey Academy of Platform Tennis

MASON / CHARTER NEW YORK 1977

FIRST EDITION

Library of Congress Cataloging in Publication Data

Ballard, Bill, 1928 -
    The illustrated guide to platform tennis.

    1. Paddle tennis. I. Hevener, Jim, 1927 joint author. II. Title
GV1006.B3   796.34'6   77-24688
ISBN 0-88405-616-3
ISBN 0-88405-617-1 pbk.

2031085

Pleasant Valley Paddle Club
in West Orange, N.J.
Home of the New Jersey Academy of Platform Tennis

CONTENTS

WHY WE DID THIS BOOK

We planned the book for beginners and intermediates. By intermediates we mean players who think they ought to be coming along faster than they are. Every stroke is taken apart and described movement by movement. Instead of photographs to look at you have the Stroke Doctor. So instead of wishing you had x-ray eyes to see through the player's sweater and figure out how the arm and shoulder were turning, you have a simple wooden model to study. Besides, most books are 90% words and 10% pictures, and when you're trying to learn something you want the accent on "show" not on "tell."

In order to encourage reader participation we included tests at the end of each chapter. How else can you tell whether you learned the day's lesson or merely read it?

We borrowed the idea of troubleshooting from automobile repair manuals. We figure that if you have a problem you'd like to be able to know what's causing it without having to leaf through a whole book for the answer.

And because we understand that not everyone has what it takes to play with classic form, we worked a good deal of pragmatism into the book's teaching philosophy. You not only get the orthodox way to play the shots, but also alternatives. If one doesn't work for you, something else might and we feel you ought to know about it.

Finally, because paddle is a game and because Jim is a born cartoonist and because I still have this childhood fantasy about Ring Lardner, we've tried to make the book as much fun as possible. I hope it comes out like it went in.

Bill Ballard

Jim Hevener

P.S. If you have any questions, please contact us at Pleasant Valley Paddle Club, PO Box 421, W. Orange, N.J. 07052. Or call (201) 325-0350

THE
GAME

WHAT THE GAME IS ALL ABOUT

You can get a fair understanding of the play of the game by observing a single, typical point. That's because in good play each individual point can last a minute or longer, and can include virtually every shot in the book.

It will enhance your perception of the game if you read the following description several times. The first time through read only the **numbered** paragraphs. These are the shots being hit and will give you a play-by-play.

The second time through read down the column marked ''The Serving Team'' and imagine yourself on the court in their shoes. Afterwards, read the column marked ''The Receiving Team'' for an insight into their strategy and tactics.

The third time through read the entire description alternating back and forth from offense to defense. This will give you insights about anticipation, on-court response, reactions and attitudes in the overall context of a point.

Ready? Play!

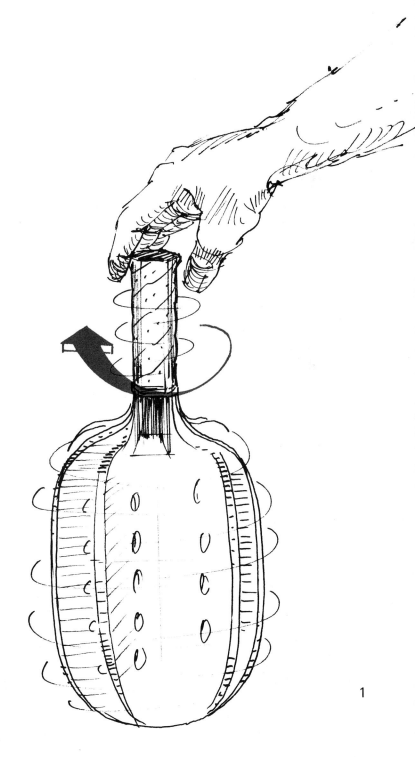

THE GAME

THE SERVING TEAM

Preparation:
The server, S, takes a position that gives the best angle for placing the serve to the receiver's backhand. Server's partner, SP, takes a position about an arm's length from the net in the ready position with the paddle up.

S bounces the ball a few times to compose himself, looks up to make certain that R is ready to receive.

1. **SERVICE:** S delivers a spinning ball fairly deep and towards the backhand of R.

(S runs to the net behind his shot, stopping near midcourt just as R is about to make his return.)

3. **APPROACH VOLLEY:** From a secure position S volleys the ball low and deep to R's backhand.

(After volleying, S continues toward the net until he is parallel to SP)

THE RECEIVING TEAM

Preparation:
The receiver, R, takes a position that gives the best chance to avoid hitting a backhand return. Receiver's partner, RP, stands back at the baseline, even with R. His job is to judge whether the service lands in the box and if it does not, to call it OUT.

(As S serves, R runs around his backhand by stepping closer to the centermark.)

2. **RETURN OF SERVICE:** R hits a topspin forehand drive down the middle where the net is at its lowest.

(R recovers from his follow-through and bounces into the ready position for the next shot.)

4. **BACKHAND LOB:** R aims the ball up the middle of the court between S and SP, thus minimizing the risk of error.

(AT THIS POINT ALL FOUR PLAYERS ARE IN GOOD POSITIONS AND ARE PREPARED TO PLAY OUT AN INDEFINITE RALLY)

5. **OVERHEAD:** SP calls MINE, since the ball is on his forehand, and hits a medium pace overhead crosscourt deep into RP's corner screens.

(After the hit SP moves back closer to the net even with S.)

(RP anticipates a crosscourt screen shot, backs into good position. R takes good position to handle the alternative of an overhead to the middle.)

6. **BLOCK LOB:** RP intercepts the ball to prevent its going into the corner. He lobs it with his backhand, crosscourt.

2

7. OVERHEAD: SP calls MINE and hits again into the corner of RP.
(SP anticipates another lob and so hangs back instead of moving in closer to the net again.)

9. OVERHEAD: SP backs way up for this deep lob. To play safe he hits a fairly soft shot down the middle.

(SP was really stretched out to make the overhead and is careless about closing in towards the net.)

11. OVERHEAD: S backs up, calls for the ball, jumps up and hits crosscourt to R's corner. His style is to hit somewhat harder than his partner does.
(Both S and SP sense that they are vulnerable. S momentarily regrets not having hit his overhead to the middle which would have been slightly safer.)

13. SCREEN SHOT - LOB: SP scrambles back past the baseline, retrieves the ball off the back screen, and sends up a desperation lob.
(S and SP are now in the defensive position. SP regretting that he failed to zone laterally and thereby left the alley open for R to drive his passing shot.)

(RP anticipates another overhead to his corner.)

8. SCREEN SHOT - BACKHAND LOB: RP permits ball to carom off side screen into back screen. To help him out, R calls TWO, meaning "two wire shot."
(Having hit a good, deep lob RP considers the possibility that a weak overhead may be forthcoming. Since this would be on his forehand he is alert for a chance to drive.)

10. LOB: The overhead bounces rather deep and low so the defenders permit it to go to the back wire. RP calls MINE and purposefully throws up a forehand lob to S, hoping to break up the net team's rhythm.
(Both R and RP sense a possible turnover now. S and SP are deeper than they should be. If the ball comes out off the screen, R will drive it.)

12. SCREEN SHOT - FOREHAND DRIVE: R takes the ball off the side wire and hits a passing shot down the line.

(Both R and RP charge to the net behind the passing shot. They have become the offensive team.)

14. OVERHEAD: RP calls MINE and spanks the ball sharply downward so that it will make a high arc and be on its way downward by the time it lands in the crosscourt side screen.

3

15. SCREEN SHOT - LOB: SP scrapes the ball off the side wire rather than letting it go to the second wire. He hits another weak lob.

(SP bounces off the wire and re-covers to a better defensive position rather than leave the middle unguarded.)

17. SCREEN SHOT - LOB: SP floats under the ball and hits a lovely, deep lob that sails over the head of both net players.

(Both S and SP advance to the net again and retake the offensive.)

19. LET GO BY: S and SP are watching the face of R's paddle as he winds up. As the drive comes flying back at them they step aside to avoid it. The ball continues past them into the back screen without bouncing. Point over.

(Even though he knows he has hit a fine shot RP does not relax his concentration, but expects the ball to be returned.)

16. OVERHEAD: RP hits the ball back to SP again but angles it so that it will bounce off the back screen and then out to the side screen.

(There is a moment of uncertainty, confusion as to who will hit this ball. Nobody calls for it. They both realize it is too late. They retreat hastily to the back screen.)

18. BACKHAND DRIVE OFF THE SCREEN: Angry with himself for not having put either of the two short lobs away, R becomes impatient. When the ball caroms off the back wire he lashes at it with his backhand.

(Although he knows the point is all but lost, R still has the hope that S or SP may flag the ball and keep it in play, so he recovers to the ready position.)

Now that you've followed a point and observed its cat-and-mouse quality, you probably have lots of questions. The chapters to come will give you the answers. With lots of interruptions and asides to liven up the learning process.

Go to it!

4 KEY POSITIONS

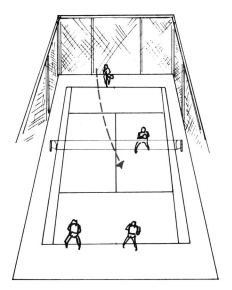

SERVICE
Server behind baseline, partner at net. Both defenders back near their baseline.

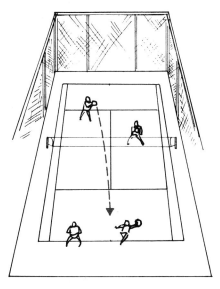

FIRST VOLLEY
Server rushes net; stops mid-court to volley. Partner does not back away.

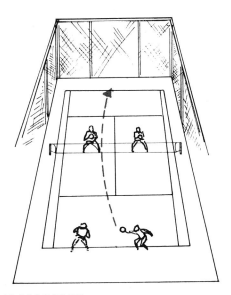

RALLYING
Two up - two back. Offensive team makes wall at net. Defenders probe.

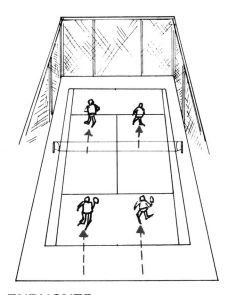

TURNOVER
Both offensive players retreat and both defensive players move up to net.

Rx: THINK WITH YOUR BODY

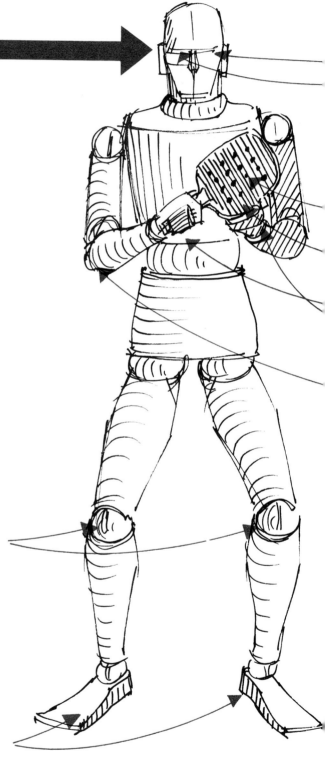

You're looking at the Stroke Doctor. He's made of wood but he's no dummy. Like you, he has hinges all over his body. The better to show you how to move on the court. Because he has no brain, the Stroke Doctor has no worries, is never tense, and does all his thinking with his body. You do the same and it will do wonders for your game.

Let's observe all those body basics. When you think you've got them down, stand in front of a full length mirror. If the images match, you're on your way.

Knees: bent enough so that your waist is about 6 inches lower than normal. Be comfortably crouched.

Feet: outside the line of your shoulders. This gives you a solid base. Keep your weight on the soles of your feet, not your heels.

6

Eyes: mostly on the ball. Also, size up the opponent's positions on the court. Watch the face of the hitter's paddle. It is not necessary, and may even be counterproductive to watch your partner hitting the ball.

Head: slightly forward. In the same plane as your backbone.

Paddle: up about shoulder-high. Not directly in front of your face, but to one side of your body's centerline.

Paddle: favoring the backhand. Face slightly open.

Gripping hand: holding tight.

Other hand: bracing the paddle.

Waist: bent forward. Lean a little but not so much that you feel as if you'll topple.

Elbows: bent naturally. Pointing down like elbows, not out like chicken wings.

Wrist: locked.

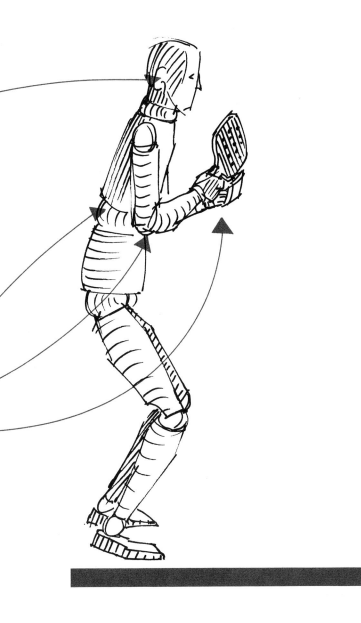

Body location: no more than 4 feet away from the net when in the volleying position. No more than a foot or two behind the baseline when defending.

To pivot for a stroke: lift up the foot that is on the same side that the ball is coming to; turn it so the toe points at the side screen; rest your body weight entirely on that rear foot.

SERVICE

WHAT SERVING IS ALL ABOUT

Since you get only one serve in paddle a certain amount of mental toughness is required. It doesn't pay to get spooked into serving a meatball because you're afraid of serving a fault. So, although consistency is important, if you get all your serves in without ever faulting, the chances are pretty good that you are not doing enough with the ball. It is not sufficient to get the ball in the court. You must also try to get something on the ball, because if you don't, the offensive balance will swing over to the receiver. And if serving is about anything, it is about staying on the offensive.

In order to get something on the ball you will have to put everything you have into the serve. That does not mean all the power you have; it means all the parts of your body.

You want to have your weight moving forward as you hit. You want to have your wrist snapping the paddle into the ball. You want to have your hitting arm feel as if it was throwing the paddle at the ball, not merely pushing at it. And finally you want to have your legs moving you forward into the best position for your first volley. You should not think of the service being completed until you are hitting that first volley.

The mechanics you'll find on the next few pages. But the strategy is worth getting into right now.

First and foremost, think offense. Not aces. They are rare. But always try to provoke defensive returns so that you can get to the net comfortably and carry on with the business of controlling the play. An offensive serve is invariably deep. Preferably with spin on it. Ideally to the receiver's backhand or right into his body so that his return is not an offensive stroke. Good players will move the ball around somewhat so the receiver can't dig in.

HIT ^{UP} NOT DOWN

Appearances are deceiving. You may think you have to hit down on the ball to serve it into the box. Wrong. That is geometrically impossible. What really happens is that your paddle hits the ball just below its equator. The wrist snap and the arm motion and the followthrough then take over. To prove that you must hit up at the

and to the right all at the same time, and at the peak of the hill you will start to go down.

To help you get the concept clear, imagine that you had to serve the ball over a wall just a few feet in front of you. The ball will be pulled down into the service box by spin, gravity and its own deceleration. And don't make the mistake of trying to skim the ball over the net cord. Try to clear it by a couple of

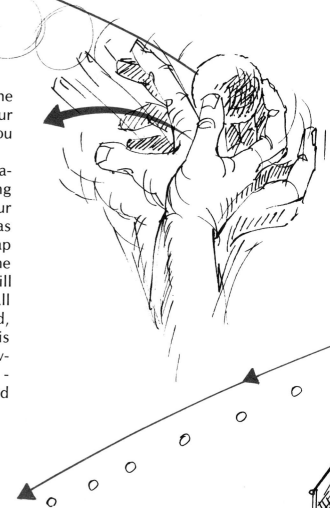

ball, kneel at the service line and serve. It can be done if your mechanics are good. But if you hit down, no way.

Bear in mind that a combination of motions are all taking place at the same time: your paddle is moving upward as well as forward; the wrist snap will bring it out and around the ball; the followthrough will continue it across and down. All of this combines to give speed, spin, depth and direction. If this sounds complex, imagine driving your car on an uphill curve - you are going forward, upward feet. A ball with an arc will fall nicely into the box. A ball with no arc will be long or short depending entirely on how hard you hit it.

The best position to serve from is the one that gives you the best shot at your target. If you stand too wide, that is too near the alley when serving from the right court, you will not have a good line to the receiver's backhand. Conversely, if you stand too near the center when serving from the left court, your partner's head may block your view of the target area. Although serving, more than any other stroke, offers the widest range of styles, generally it is more convenient to stand nearer to the center when serving from the right court than when serving from the left court.

After you have delivered your serve follow the line of the ball to the net. Do not run to the net on a line parallel to the sideline. That will put you in a bad position to hit your first volley. The return, if it is a drive, will most likely be aimed at the center of the net, so that is the line of approach you should take.

One final thought. The serve is the easiest of all strokes to practice because you can do it by yourself. And since a service fault is an instant loser, this is the stroke that you really ought to work on. The other team can beat you with volleys and overheads and drives and lobs, but the service is the stroke that lets you beat yourself.

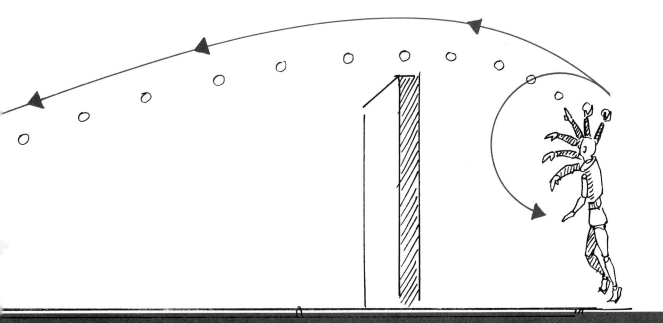

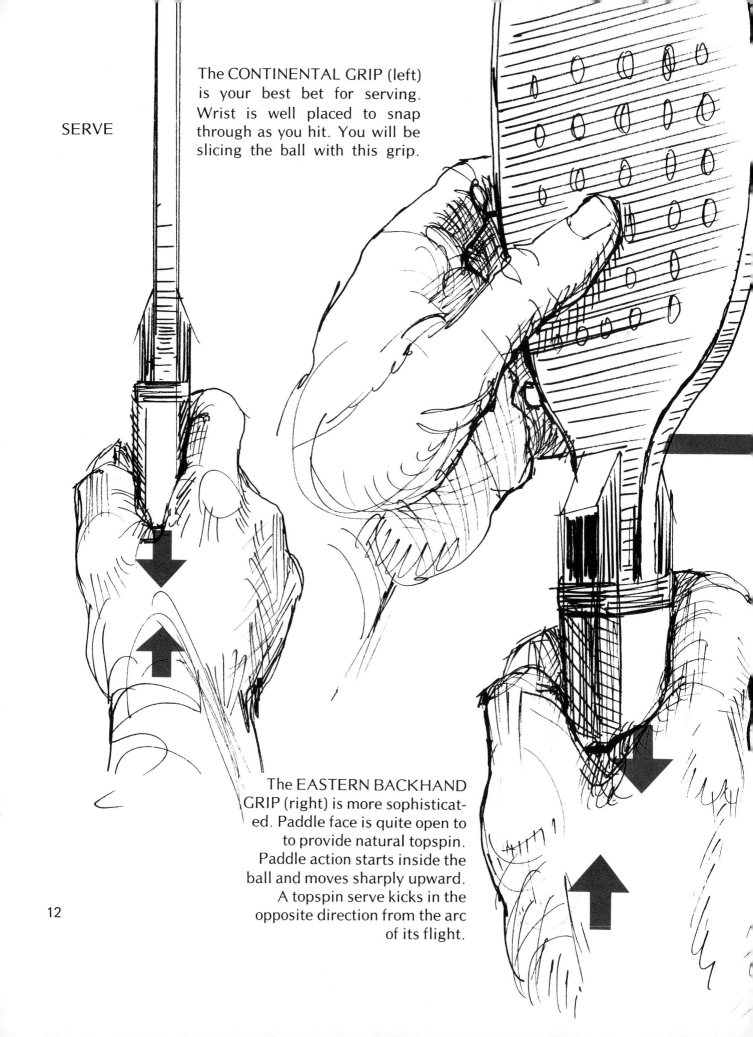

SERVE

The CONTINENTAL GRIP (left) is your best bet for serving. Wrist is well placed to snap through as you hit. You will be slicing the ball with this grip.

The EASTERN BACKHAND GRIP (right) is more sophisticated. Paddle face is quite open to to provide natural topspin. Paddle action starts inside the ball and moves sharply upward. A topspin serve kicks in the opposite direction from the arc of its flight.

FINGERTIP CONTROL

The toss is really a lifting motion. Treat the ball like a hollow egg shell. Use thumb and first two fingers only. Avoid palming the ball or squeezing it. Gently does it. Toss ball two feet out into the court and a foot or so out to the side (for a slice); toss ball straight ahead to hit a flatter serve; toss ball overhead and arch your back to hit with topspin or twist. How high the toss? Six inches higher than you can reach with the tip of your paddle when your arm is fully extended. Wait with the paddle poised for ball to drop into striking zone and then throw the full weight of the paddle up at the ball.

SERVE

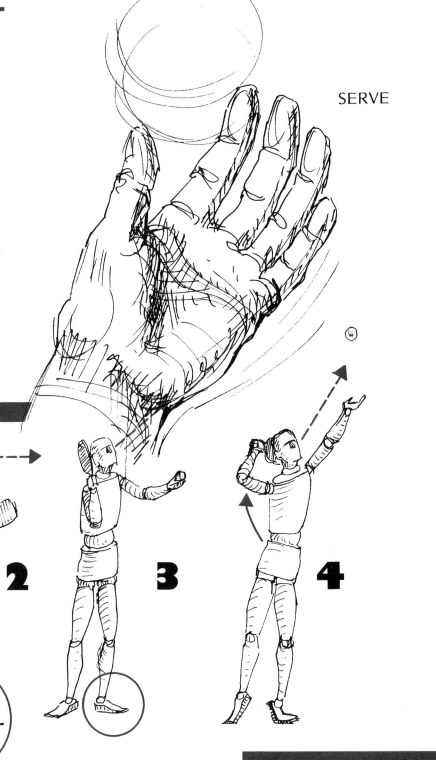

1. **RELAX.** Bounce ball. Check feet. Be sure receiver is ready.

2. **CHECK TARGET.** Paddle and ball together. Weight well balanced.

3. **IN MOTION.** Cock paddle back. Look up. Weight forward. Toss.

4. **EXTEND YOURSELF.** Elbow up. Head up. Up on toes. Lean into shot.

13

POWER PLOY

SERVE

1. Fully-cocked elbow on the backswing looks like, works like a pitcher's windup. Going off half-cocked amounts to slapping the ball instead of stroking it.

2. Moving body weight forward with stroke multiplies power-thrust. Holding body back sets up opposing forces within your own body.

3. Maximum extension of arm upward at ball makes contact occur at point of maximum acceleration. Lower toss would reduce your crack-the-whip effect.

4. Wrist-snap at contact prolongs interface of ball and paddle, adds spin and heaviness to ball. Failure to snap wrist results in a jab-like punch instead of a long, flowing hook.

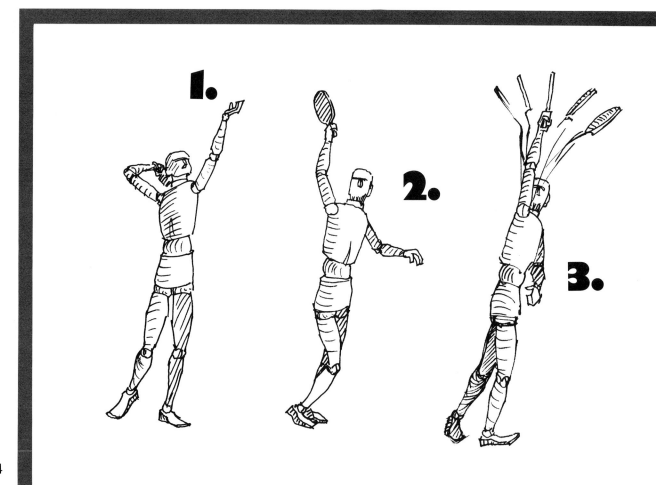

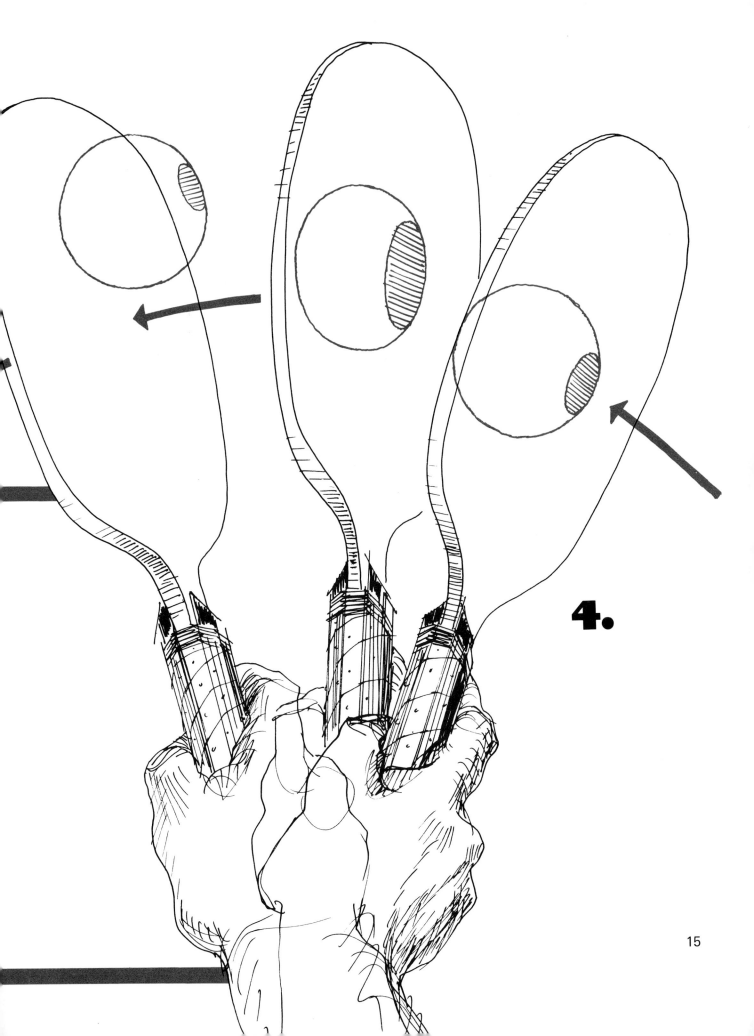

4.

SERVE

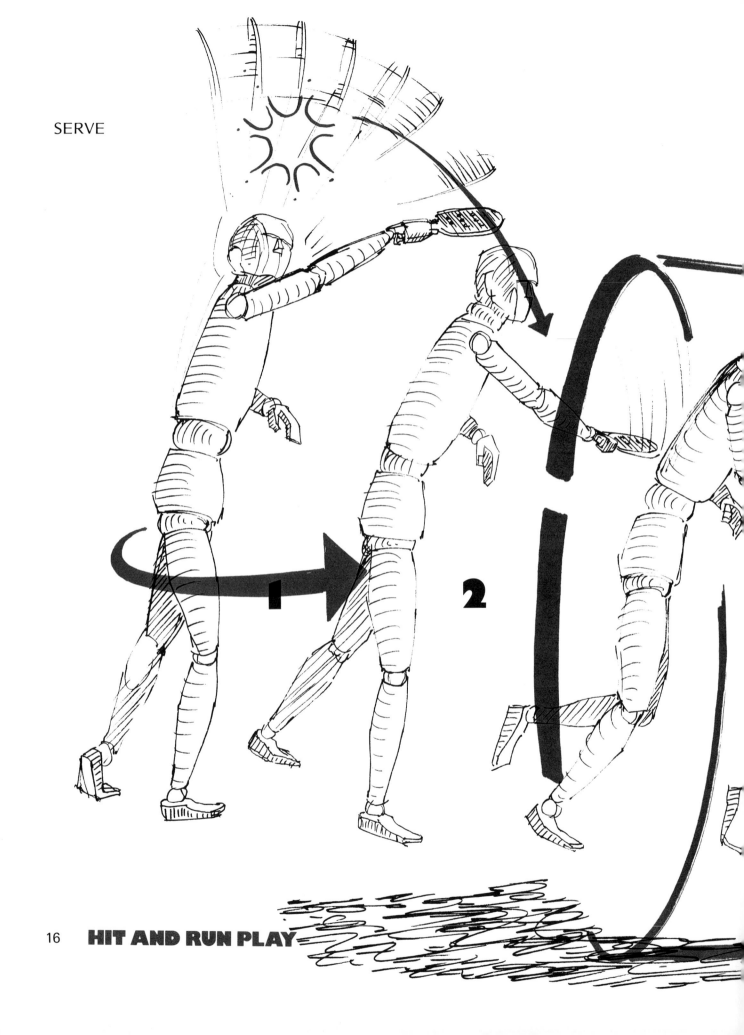

1

2

HIT AND RUN PLAY

The service is a sequence of actions that does not end until you have hit your first volley. Action 1 is the hit itself. The back leg swings over the baseline as you run (2) toward the net along the line of your serve. As you recover from your followthrough (3) you run ''into the cup'' keeping low to handle the low drive return of service. By stage 4 your paddle is up in front of you, and your body is down as the receiver is about to hit the service back. At the last possible moment you come to a stop, feet apart, and set up to hit the first volley. You are at least up to the service line, a few feet closer if you can manage it.

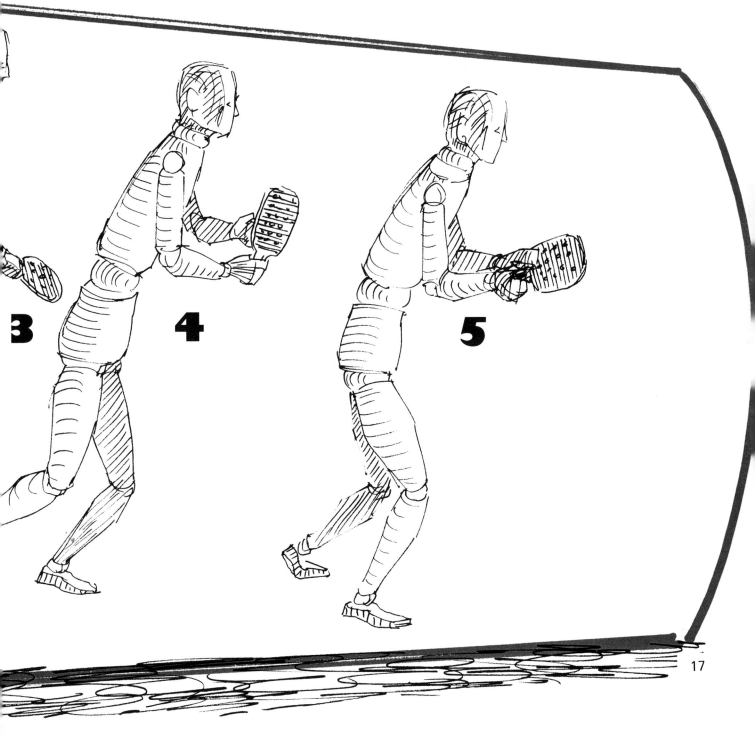

TROUBLESHOOTING THE SERVICE

How to use the **TROUBLESHOOT-ING SECTION.** First, identify the specific problem you are having. Then relate the NUMBERS in the column opposite your problem to the possible DIAGNOSES listed below. By the process of elimination you will arrive at the cause or causes of your PROBLEM.

Problem	Diagnoses
Serving into the net	4, 6, 7, 10, 11, 13, 15, 16
Serving long	4, 6, 10, 13, 15, 16
Serving wide	3, 8, 10, 12, 15
Serving short	4, 6, 10, 11, 13, 15, 17
Popping ball up	4, 6, 8, 10, 11, 13, 15, 17
Lack of power	1, 2, 4, 6, 8, 11, 13, 14, 15, 17
Swing and miss	1, 5, 7, 10, 15
Off-center hits	1, 5, 10, 12, 15, 16
No spin, flat serve	8, 9, 11, 12, 13, 14
High % of faults	1, 3, 4, 7, 10, 11, 15, 16

1. Too complicated a windup
2. Not enough elbow-cock
3. Poor starting position
4. Tossing too low
5. Tossing to high
6. Tossing too close
7. Tossing too far forward
8. No wrist snap
9. Not using Continental grip
11. Lack of concentration
11. Not hitting up and through
12. Forearm turned the wrong way
13. No followthrough
14. No shoulder turn
15. Not watching ball
16. Trying too hard/swinging too fast
17. No weight behind stroke

TESTING THE SERVICE

Serve 5 balls from the right court. Each ball must land in the service box. Ditto from the left court. Start again - this time each ball must land in the back half of the targeted service box. When you accomplish this at least 4 out of 5 hits, start again. This time hit 4 to area 3, then one to area 4. Then 4 to area 1 and one to area 2. This ratio, 3 to the backhand corner for every one to the forehand corner is about right.

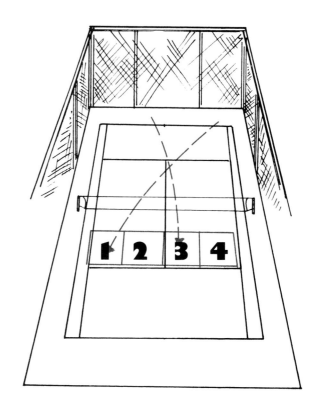

QUIZ

1. The least important attribute of a serve is (speed, consistency, placement).

2. For variety a good idea is to (serve a surprise underhand serve, serve right at the receiver to jam him, stay at the baseline and don't come to the net).

3. The proper action in hitting the ball is (down and across, up and through, around and about).

4. The most useful service grip is (the Western, the Eastern Forehand, the Continental).

5. If you never, never serve a fault (you probably have a very good serve, you probably should try serving the ball harder, your serves are landing very close to the lines).

6. The best servers usually do not serve (with sidespin, with topspin, flat).

7. Power in the serve does **not** come from (body weight, uncocking of the paddle arm, knee flexion).

8. The major factor in spinning the ball is (followthrough, paddle action, the toss).

9. It is true that (you should toss the ball before you take your backswing, if you swing and miss you get another chance, aces are uncommon).

10. You should try to hit the ball (on its way up, on its way down, exactly at the peak of the toss).

FOREHAND

3

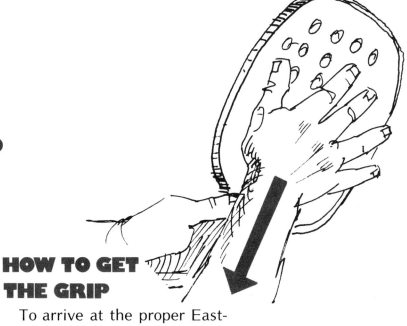

WHAT THE FOREHAND IS ALL ABOUT

In tennis the forehand drive is commonly used as a rallying stroke to keep the opponent at the baseline. Not so in paddle. In paddle the forehand is the basic offensive weapon of the defensive team, used to try to force errors or turnovers.

There simply is no such thing in paddle as a baseline-to-baseline rally. In fact there is no such playing situation as all four players in their backcourts. There is always one team at the net and the other team back. It would be poor strategy for the deep team to do nothing but try to blast the ball through the net team, unless the net team can't volley at all.

The forehand drive is best employed (1) as the return of service, (2) on balls that bounce shallow in the court, and (3) in a variety of tactical situations.

(1) When returning service, position your body so that you can handle nearly any ball on your forehand side. A good drive is far and away the best return of service because it attacks the offensive team at their weakest moment - before they can get entrenched at the net. The driving return is your earliest (and may be your onliest) chance to take the offensive away from them.

(continued next page)

HOW TO GET THE GRIP

To arrive at the proper Eastern Forehand grip, place your palm flat against the back face of the paddle and slide it down the handle until you are shaking hands with it.

Checkpoints: your palm should be in the same plane as the face of the paddle; the V formed by your thumb and forefinger should be above the top plane of the handle; the butt of your palm should be against the heel of the handle.

Now since paddle handles come in all different shapes and sizes, one player's Eastern may not look like another's. But if you can lay your wrist back comfortably you probably have it right. If you can't arrive at a comfortable Eastern grip as described, either try another paddle or have your handle customized. After all, there is not much you can do about the size and shape of your hand.

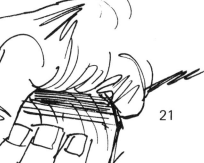

21

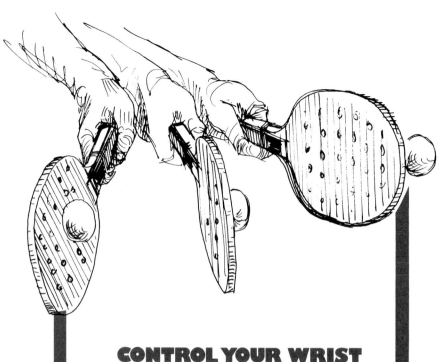

CONTROL YOUR WRIST

One key to a solid forehand drive is laying back your wrist. Once your wrist is laid back, lock it. You are **not** going to snap your wrist as you hit. You **are** going to come through the ball with a firm wrist. If you flex your wrist as you hit, your palm will no longer be in the same plane as the paddle face. Players who find it difficult to lay back the wrist usually turn out not to be using the true Eastern Forehand grip, but a grip closer to the Continental. The Continental does not readily accommodate a laid-back wrist.

If your return is really super, you can charge to the net behind it. This is blitzing. You hope to force the server to pop your return up in the air so you can punch it away. As you blitz, your partner moves to cover the center of the backcourt in case the server manages to volley your return well. If this happens, don't try to hit the ball; let your partner handle it while you recover your position in the backcourt. Even when the blitz does not work, use of the I-formation permits you to stay in the point.

When driving the service return, your best bet is to aim down the middle where the net is lowest, only 34 inches high. Occasionally you can whack one right at the net man, especially if he is a proven poacher. If you are quick enough to take the serve on the rise, you can sometimes pass the server by going for his alley.

(2) On shallow balls the player who can take the shot as a forehand should come in quickly and try to put it away, driving between the net players or right at one of them. No matter that you might be stepping in front of your partner. If it is your forehand it is your shot. And you must make shallow volleyers pay the price.

(3) Some tactical situations that call for forehand drives: against net players who stand too deep; when your team is poor at screen play and lobbing the ball will cost you the point;

as a surprise or take-a-chance shot when the score is well in your favor; on a ball that bounces wide when the net player fails to zone; on hard-hit screen shots that rebound way out into the court.

A solid and reliable forehand drive is the **sine qua non** of a great team. But a good drive must be a net-skimmer and not a tennis-style loop that clears the net by four feet. Ideally you want to get both pace and top on the ball. A flat ball can be effective only when the bounce is high enough so that the ball can be hit down on.

Never, never drive the ball merely out of impatience. Bide your time. Sooner or later you will get the shot you are looking for.

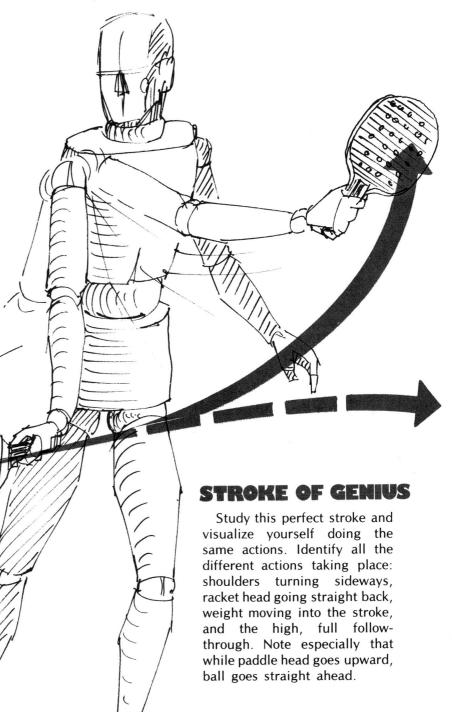

STROKE OF GENIUS

Study this perfect stroke and visualize yourself doing the same actions. Identify all the different actions taking place: shoulders turning sideways, racket head going straight back, weight moving into the stroke, and the high, full follow-through. Note especially that while paddle head goes upward, ball goes straight ahead.

23

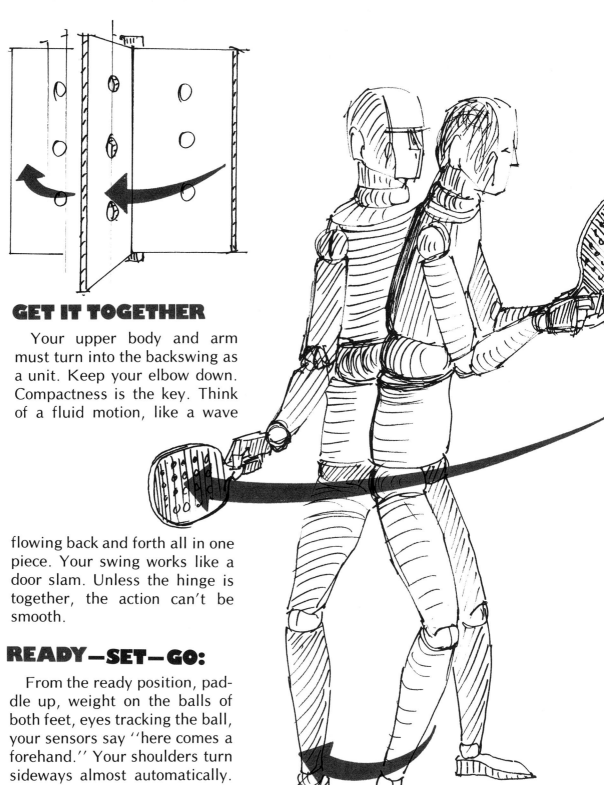

GET IT TOGETHER

Your upper body and arm must turn into the backswing as a unit. Keep your elbow down. Compactness is the key. Think of a fluid motion, like a wave flowing back and forth all in one piece. Your swing works like a door slam. Unless the hinge is together, the action can't be smooth.

READY—SET—GO:

From the ready position, paddle up, weight on the balls of both feet, eyes tracking the ball, your sensors say "here comes a forehand." Your shoulders turn sideways almost automatically. You take a small step with your back foot to shift your weight onto it. Your paddle is now pointing at the screen behind you. Your wrist has been flexed into the laid-back position. The paddle face is vertical. You are READY.

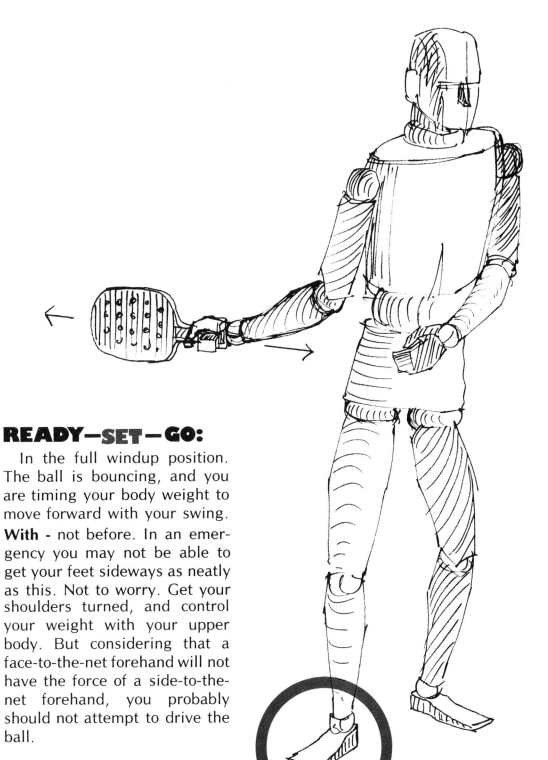

READY—SET—GO:

In the full windup position. The ball is bouncing, and you are timing your body weight to move forward with your swing. **With -** not before. In an emergency you may not be able to get your feet sideways as neatly as this. Not to worry. Get your shoulders turned, and control your weight with your upper body. But considering that a face-to-the-net forehand will not have the force of a side-to-the-net forehand, you probably should not attempt to drive the ball.

FOREHAND

READY—SET— GO:

One of the reasons for all the careful prep is to enable you to hit the ball out front. Somewhere near your front foot. Never try to drive a ball that has got past you. You may hit it off to the side. You will certainly hit with diminished power, because your weight will not be behind the shot.

In swinging through the ball, **through, not merely to,** keep your paddle face vertical. And keep your wrist firm. You will put spin on the ball by the up-ward movement of the vertically-faced paddle against the back of the ball. Don't attempt to hit with the face closed or you may risk hitting the top of the ball and driving it down instead of ahead. Some players make a slight rotation of the entire arm-wrist-paddle unit on impact. This can be effective only if the followthrough is decidedly on the high side. But it is not essential to imparting topspin. And the timing required is rather sophisticated.

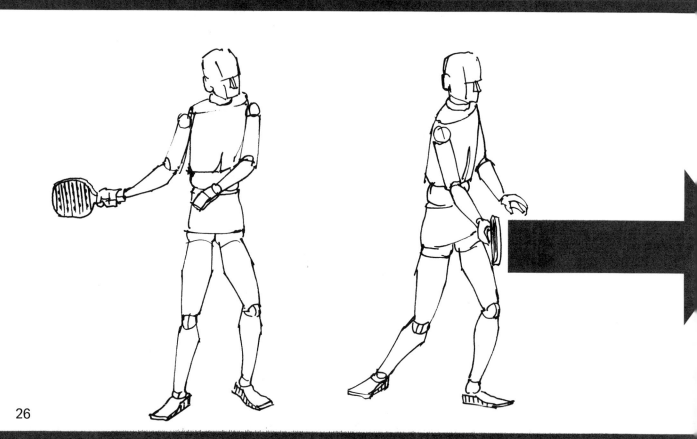

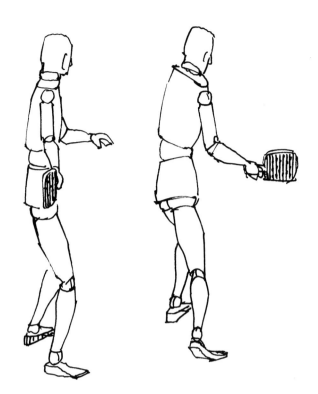

SCREEN'S EYE VIEW

Observe that as the ball is reached for, the body uncoils. Shoulders which were sideways to the net open up so that they are almost parallel to the net. Note that contact with the ball is made about thigh-high. The optimum striking zone is between waist and knee. When a ball comes to you in the absolute heart of the strike zone, and you have done a good job of preparation, you should automatically and confidently give it your best shot. Don't think. Just hit.

THE BIG FINISH

Don't make the mistake of thinking that a high finish will send the ball out of the cage. That will happen only if your paddleface is wide open. The high finish is the natural result of a free, full swing. Since the swing starts into the ball with an upward motion, an unrestricted followthrough has to continue in the same direction. The formula is UPWARD + FORWARD = TOPSPIN.

If you slow down your swing as you approach the actual hit, thereby shortening your follow-through, you will poke the ball, not stroke it. A good drive is never jerky or sudden but smooth and flowing. It actually picks up speed as it gets closer to the ball.

Note also that the weight has been transferred from the back foot to the front foot. Many beginners are tempted to step around the shot with the back foot, using the front foot as a pivot. This can result in striking the side of the ball farthest from the body, instead of the back of the ball. Result: ball flies off the paddle at an angle and goes into the side screen.

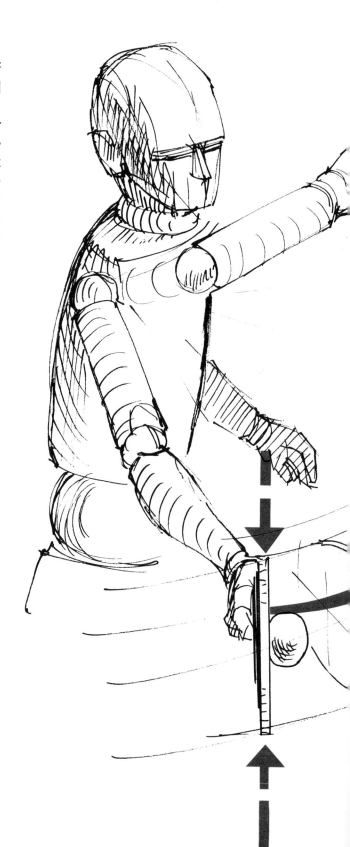

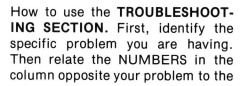

How to use the **TROUBLESHOOTING SECTION.** First, identify the specific problem you are having. Then relate the NUMBERS in the column opposite your problem to the possible DIAGNOSES listed below. By the process of elimination you will arrive at the cause or causes of your PROBLEM.

Problem	Diagnoses
Driving into the net	3, 4, 5, 9, 10, 11, 12, 14, 16, 20
Driving long	1, 2, 9, 10, 11, 19
Driving wide	6, 7, 8, 9, 10, 12, 15, 16, 18, 19
Hitting up	2, 10, 12, 16
Off-center hits	1, 4, 10, 18
Lack of power	2, 4, 6, 7, 8, 12, 15, 16, 19
Missing ball	1, 5, 8, 9, 10, 13, 17
Poor timing	1, 10, 13, 16

1. Taking too much backswing
2. Paddle face too open
3. Paddle face too closed
4. Limp wrist, loose grip
5. Not bending knees
6. Stepping with wrong foot
7. Standing too close to ball
8. Standing too far from ball
9. Swinging too hard/flat
10. Not watching ball
11. Trying for too many winners
12. No followthrough
13. Not ready/not recovering
14. Swinging down not out
15. Not hitting out front
16. Weight back, not forward
17. Not concentrating
18. Paddle face angled sideways
19. Hitting too far out front
20. Taking too high a backswing

TESTING-FOREHAND DRIVE

Position yourself at either A or D. Hit 5 balls over the net so they land between the baseline and the service line. Do this a few times, picking up the pace a little each time. When you get 10 in without a miss, start going for the specific targets 1, 2 and 3. After you become proficient at this, get a friend to feed you the balls so that you have to run to get to them. Work on this drill so that you develop complete confidence in the stroke.

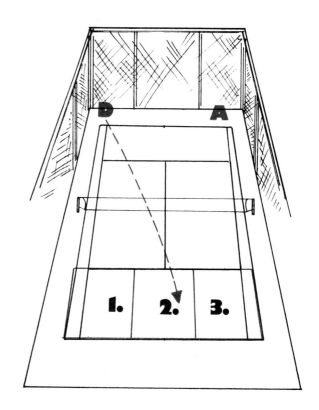

QUIZ

1. The forehand drive is (a secondary stroke, essential for a strong game, the best shot when caught deep behind the baseline).

2. The wrist should be (laid back, cocked, above the paddle head).

3. The Eastern Forehand Grip is (not as closed as the Continental, also called the hatchet grip, most effective to obtain top).

4. Drives should clear the net (with three feet to spare, because of sidespin, by a couple of inches).

5. Rolling the arm and wrist as you hit (adds underspin, compensates for poor footwork, is merely an option).

6. In preparing for the shot do **not** (take a roundhouse backswing, turn sideways to the net, put weight on the back foot).

7. It is usually a good idea to (drive shallow volleys, shift grips during the backswing, let the ball drop to your ankles).

8. Forehand drives are frequently hit by (the offensive team, the defensive team, the woman in mixed doubles).

9. On the followthrough the paddle head should finish (with its striking face parallel to the deck, chest high, shoulder high or even higher).

10. Hitting late usually results in (a chop shot, a wristy shot, poor directional control).

WHY PROS GET GRAY

Because pupils expect too much of themselves too soon. Rome wasn't built in a day and neither was a great forehand, let alone a great game. Be patient. Be kind to yourself. Stop analyzing your faults. Give your pro a chance to earn his money.

Because pupils don't practice between lessons. Imagine taking dancing, driving or typing lessons and not practicing in between. Madness. Would a computer expert program a machine and then never run the program?

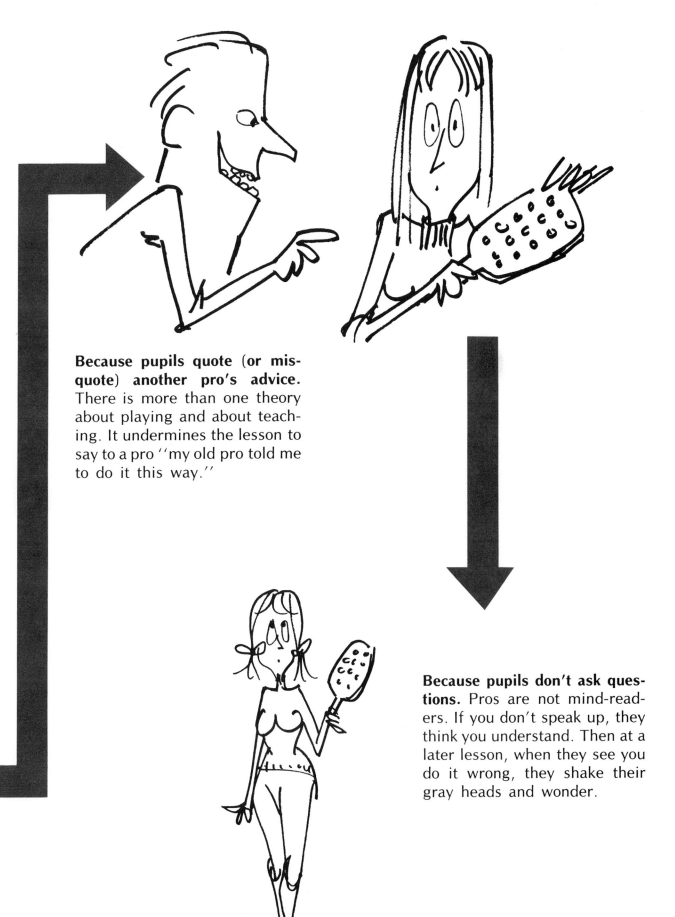

Because pupils quote (or misquote) another pro's advice. There is more than one theory about playing and about teaching. It undermines the lesson to say to a pro "my old pro told me to do it this way."

Because pupils don't ask questions. Pros are not mind-readers. If you don't speak up, they think you understand. Then at a later lesson, when they see you do it wrong, they shake their gray heads and wonder.

THE VOLLEY

WHAT VOLLEYING IS ALL ABOUT

A volley is a return of the ball before it bounces. Not to be confused with a rally which is an exchange of shots during the play. When people say ''volley for serve'' they mean to say ''rally.''

The volley is more common in paddle than in tennis for a number of reasons. For one thing there is **always** one team at the net position, responding to the other team's drives with volleys. There is simply no such thing in paddle as a baseline-to-baseline rally. Also, in tennis the volley is often a putaway while in paddle it rarely ends the point.

There are about a dozen different names of volleys and they are described elsewhere, but in the simplest sense there are only two kinds of volleys - volleys that go in and volleys that do not. Form is secondary to effect.

The First Axiom of paddle is Keep The Ball In Play. So even a puny pop-fly volley serves its purpose. However, good volleyers are able to do things with the ball, keep it deep and low, so the defenders are forever pinned at their baseline hitting weak returns. Good volleying technique depends on 3 attitudes, one physical, one mental and one tactical.

The physical secret of success is HOLD TIGHT. If you don't nothing else matters. When you hit the ball with a loose grip there is no telling which way it will go. Or even if the paddle will stay in your hand. Now, the question you ask is: how tight is tight? Squeezing tight. Fist tight. Tight enough to feel the muscles in your forearm. Tighter than your service grip. A tight grip locks your wrist as well as your hand and you will need both to handle the drives coming your way. In between volleys relax your grip to avoid muscle cramps. But when the ball is on its way back to you, HOLD TIGHT.

The correct mental approach to volleying is BE FEARLESS. You can't volley well if you are a chicken at the net. You must stand your ground, much closer to the net than in tennis - belly

35

VOLLEY

up to the net in some rallies - and invite the opponents to hit right at you. In fact, the harder they drive, the closer you want to stand. You don't dare leave room between your body and the net for them to hit a dipping drive at your shoetops. But, you say, I might get hit by the ball. Yes. You will. Every good player has been. But the risk of being hit is actually less if you stand close to the net than if you flinch away or freeze at mid-court with your paddle hanging down. Few shots in paddle are more soul-satisfying than volleying an opponent's hardest drive right back at his feet for a winner. Well, maybe a winner and maybe not. And that leads to attitude number three.

The tactical approach that works best in paddle is: DON'T TRY TO DO TOO MUCH WITH YOUR VOLLEYS. This is especially true of your first volley, or approach volley. Volleying winners are rarer in paddle than in tennis because the court is small and there are always the wires to give the defenders a second chance. Do not even think about volleying the ball for a winner. Just think deep and low. Try to get the ball near the baseline and to a backhand. Give them a ball they have to lob. Give them a chance to make an error. Your volley is more often a means to an end than an end in itself. Your objective is to keep them on the defensive without risking an error. If you keep a tight grip on your paddle, hug the net, and keep the ball deep, the opportunity for winners will come.

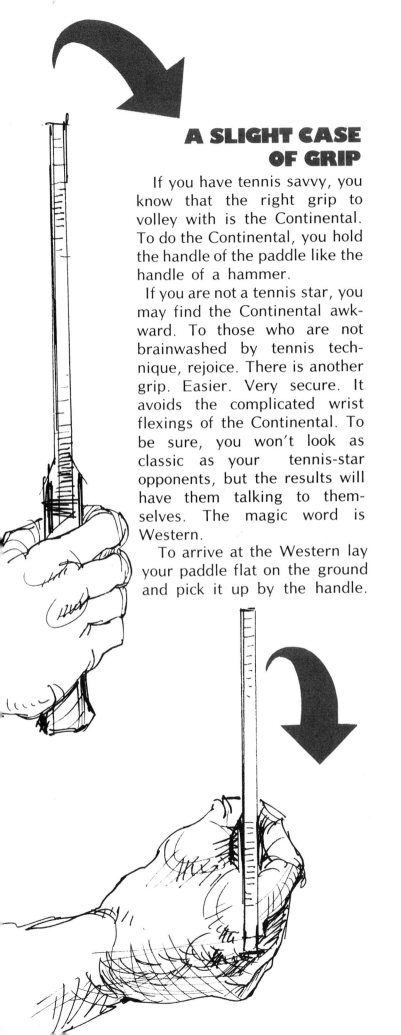

A SLIGHT CASE OF GRIP

If you have tennis savvy, you know that the right grip to volley with is the Continental. To do the Continental, you hold the handle of the paddle like the handle of a hammer.

If you are not a tennis star, you may find the Continental awkward. To those who are not brainwashed by tennis technique, rejoice. There is another grip. Easier. Very secure. It avoids the complicated wrist flexings of the Continental. To be sure, you won't look as classic as your tennis-star opponents, but the results will have them talking to themselves. The magic word is Western.

To arrive at the Western lay your paddle flat on the ground and pick it up by the handle.

Now you should be holding it pretty much like a fly swatter, and indeed, your volley motion is going to be something like a swat. Not classic for sure, but oh so effective. Especially for people who are afraid of playing the net. It seems that the Western just naturally makes you feel safer. Only one thing to remember: you are going to hit every volley using only one face of the paddle.

On balls that come right at you, react with a natural push-away motion. Hold the paddle head straight up like a giant lollipop and push. On the backhand side push the paddle into the ball with your knuckles pointing up. On your forehand side, turn the paddle handle like you would turn a doorknob. Now your knuckles are pointing down and you push the paddle into the ball with the same pallde face. Use your free hand on the rim of the paddle to brace for the backhand volley.

With a Western you can make good use of your wrist to get extra depth. On higher balls your wrist will enable you to get both power and spin, especially if you snap the paddle across the back of the ball.

You may fall in love with the Western. Or you may hate it. It is a minority grip, no question. But it can be devastating because of the extra power you get when your entire wrist is behind the handle.

37

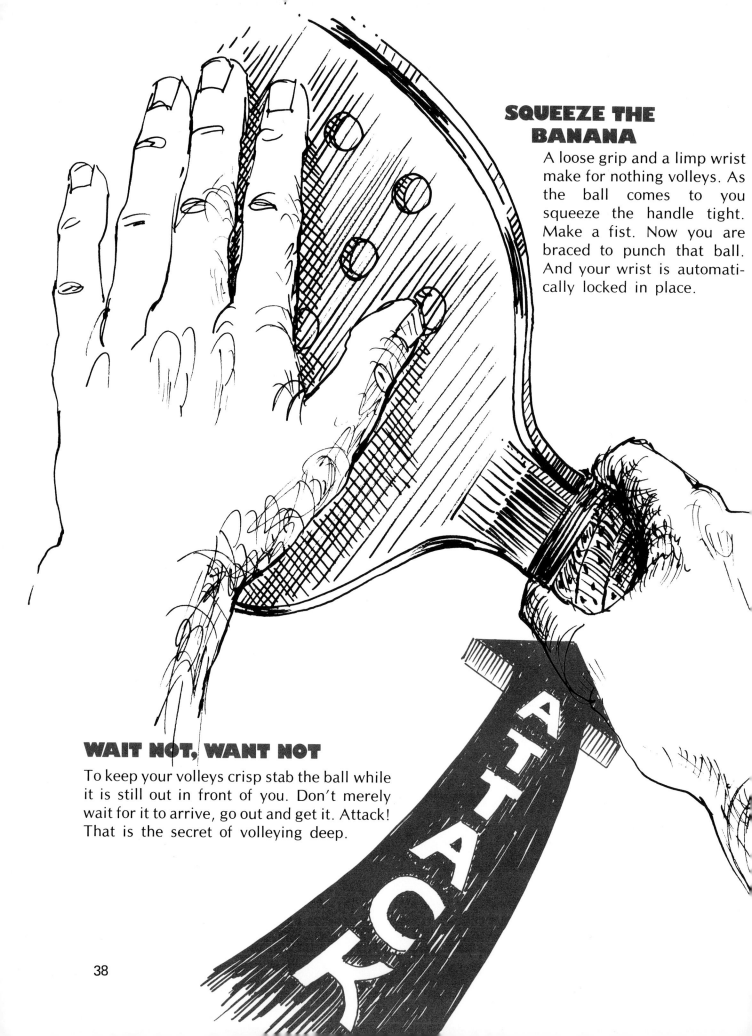

SQUEEZE THE BANANA

A loose grip and a limp wrist make for nothing volleys. As the ball comes to you squeeze the handle tight. Make a fist. Now you are braced to punch that ball. And your wrist is automatically locked in place.

WAIT NOT, WANT NOT

To keep your volleys crisp stab the ball while it is still out in front of you. Don't merely wait for it to arrive, go out and get it. Attack! That is the secret of volleying deep.

ATTACK

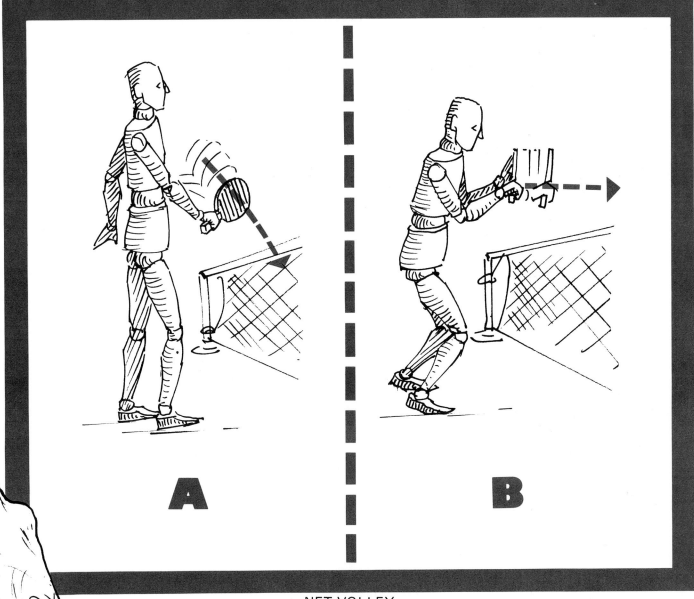

NET VOLLEY

LOWER YOUR SIGHTS... Casual player (A) is too erect, weight is back on heels. From this position player can see only the **top** of the ball. Pokes down at it and pushes it into net. If lucky, ball clears net but lands short and invites a drive. Alert player (B) is in crouch, anxious to move forward, sees the **back** of the ball and punches right through it aiming volley deep to either opponent's backhand. The instant after ball is hit, croucher bounces back into ready position (B) and is ready to volley the next shot.

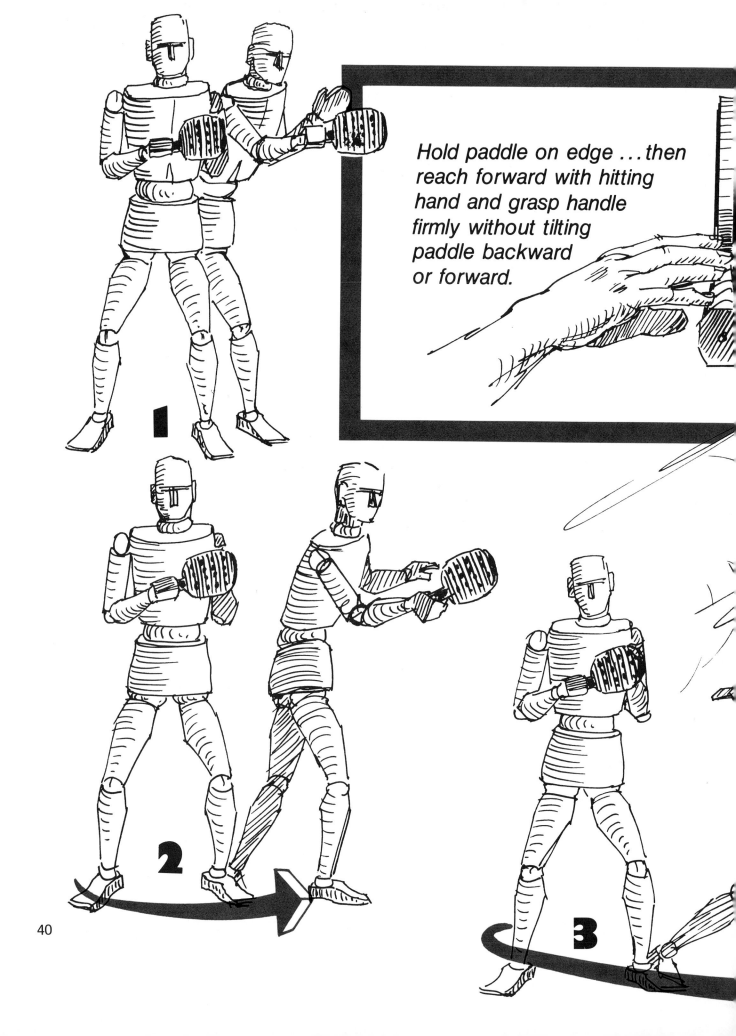

Hold paddle on edge ... then reach forward with hitting hand and grasp handle firmly without tilting paddle backward or forward.

1

2

3

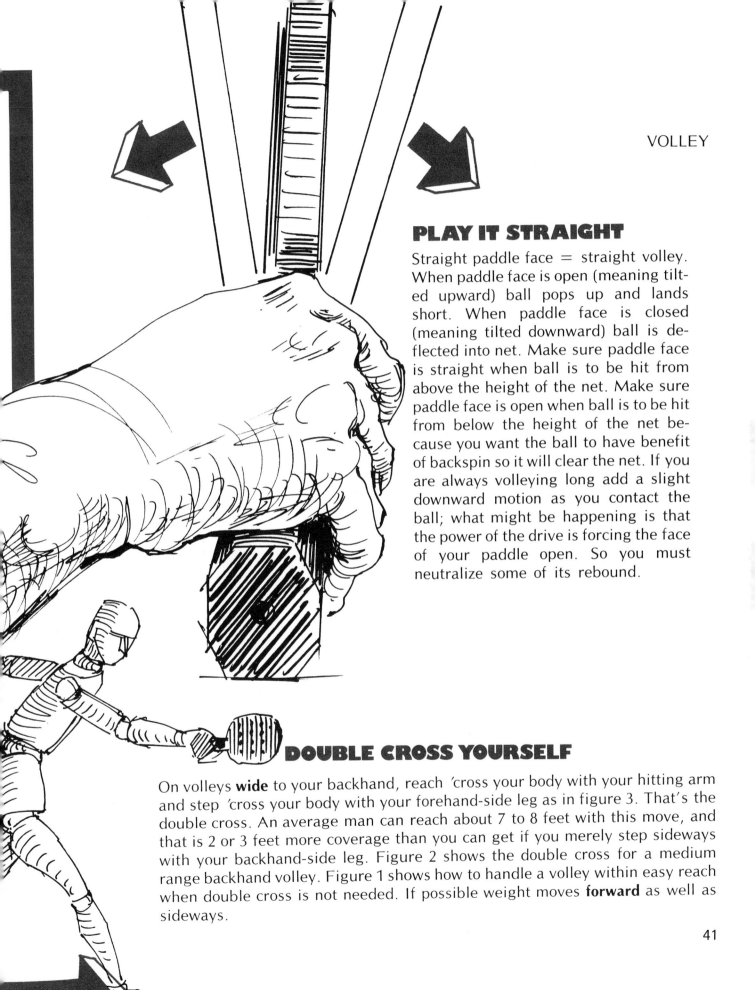

PLAY IT STRAIGHT

Straight paddle face = straight volley. When paddle face is open (meaning tilted upward) ball pops up and lands short. When paddle face is closed (meaning tilted downward) ball is deflected into net. Make sure paddle face is straight when ball is to be hit from above the height of the net. Make sure paddle face is open when ball is to be hit from below the height of the net because you want the ball to have benefit of backspin so it will clear the net. If you are always volleying long add a slight downward motion as you contact the ball; what might be happening is that the power of the drive is forcing the face of your paddle open. So you must neutralize some of its rebound.

DOUBLE CROSS YOURSELF

On volleys **wide** to your backhand, reach 'cross your body with your hitting arm and step 'cross your body with your forehand-side leg as in figure 3. That's the double cross. An average man can reach about 7 to 8 feet with this move, and that is 2 or 3 feet more coverage than you can get if you merely step sideways with your backhand-side leg. Figure 2 shows the double cross for a medium range backhand volley. Figure 1 shows how to handle a volley within easy reach when double cross is not needed. If possible weight moves **forward** as well as sideways.

41

UNDER MEANS OVER

For tennis players and more sophisticated paddlers, volleying with backspin is the preferred approach. Backspin, or underspin, is applied by hitting forward and downward with an open-faced paddle. Too much open face means a floater; too little means a shallow volley. Back the paddle slightly off the vertical and punch a few volleys until you discover the best combination of pitch, punch and direction that keeps your volleys low and deep.

When the ball is going to be hit from below the level of the net, you need more pitch. This floats the ball up and over the tape. You'll need this extra pitch when you play against hard drivers who force you to hit approach volleys from a low position near midcourt. Stay low to the ground, bending at the knees as well as the waist, and watch the ball intently.

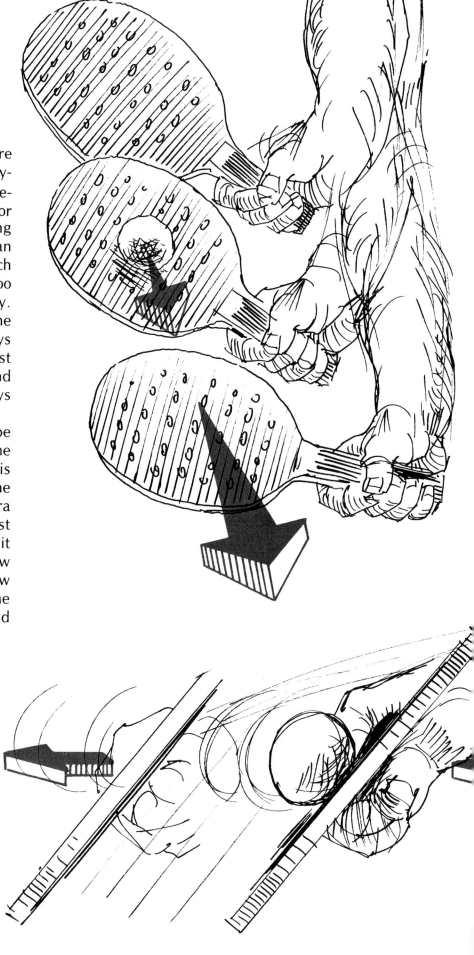

KNOW THY PARTNER AS THYSELF

You need to have a clear idea of your partner's serving ability because that determines how you will play your net position. For example, if partner has a strong service, expect a lot of lob returns and play a little deeper. If partner serves lollipops, dig in and expect to get blasted at. After a few games you should get to know the opponents too. If they like to drive down the alley, go stand there. If they chip their returns, compensate for it. You can work out verbal or finger signals for poaching or other set plays. Mostly you must know which of you is going to handle those drives down the middle. If you are equal in skill, try this formula: **low** drives to be hit by net player with backhand volley; **shoulder high** balls to be hit by player with forehand volley.

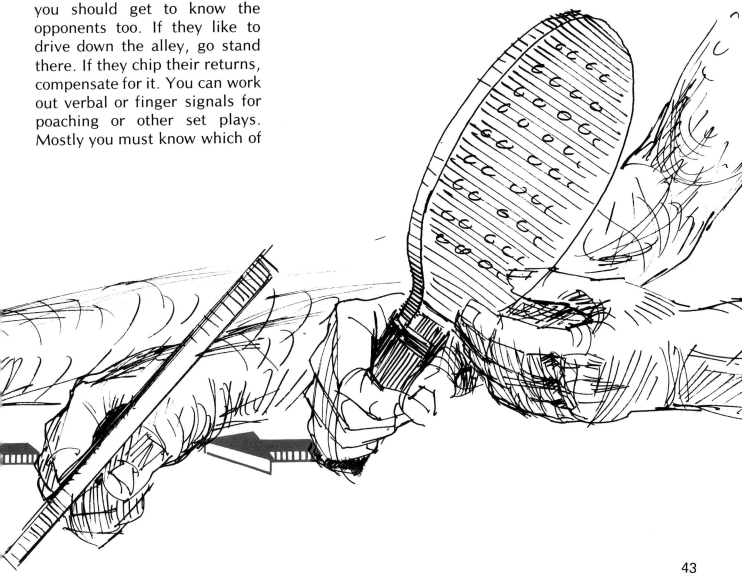

THE DROP VOLLEY

Cradle method. For forehand drop and stop volleys. At contact with ball turn wrist and forearm so that paddle curls around the bottom of the ball, taking off its motion. Ball should almost slide off paddle and drop down.

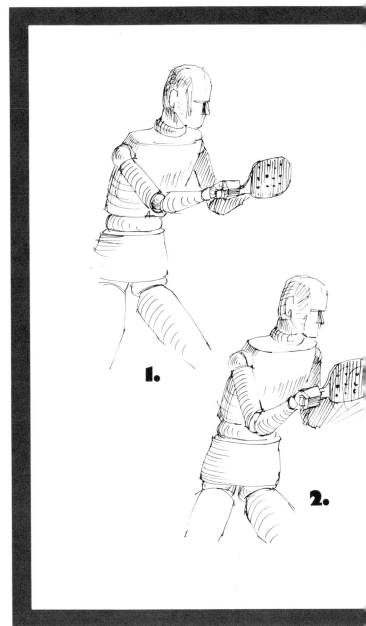

1.

2.

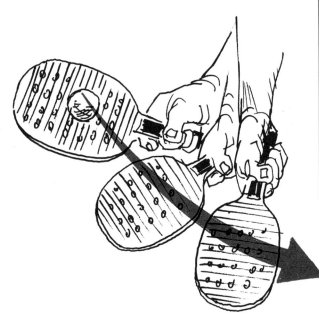

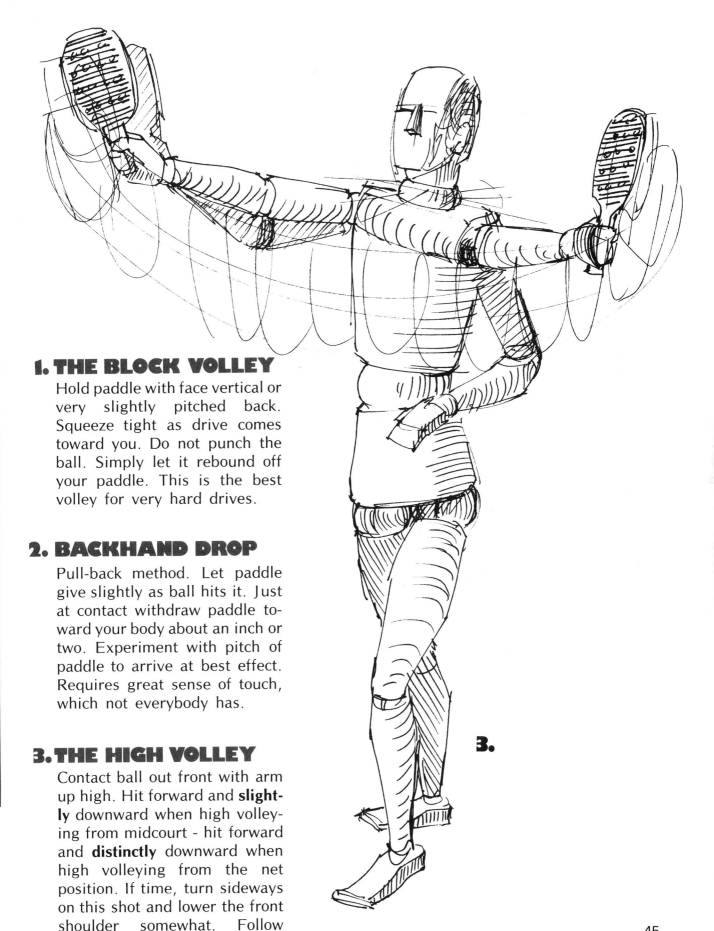

1. THE BLOCK VOLLEY

Hold paddle with face vertical or very slightly pitched back. Squeeze tight as drive comes toward you. Do not punch the ball. Simply let it rebound off your paddle. This is the best volley for very hard drives.

2. BACKHAND DROP

Pull-back method. Let paddle give slightly as ball hits it. Just at contact withdraw paddle toward your body about an inch or two. Experiment with pitch of paddle to arrive at best effect. Requires great sense of touch, which not everybody has.

3. THE HIGH VOLLEY

Contact ball out front with arm up high. Hit forward and **slightly** downward when high volleying from midcourt - hit forward and **distinctly** downward when high volleying from the net position. If time, turn sideways on this shot and lower the front shoulder somewhat. Follow through at least several feet.

3.

APPROACHING THE APPROACH VOLLEY

Depending on who tells you, the approach volley or first volley, is either hit on the dead run on your way to the net - or - just as the returner is about to whack your serve back, you stop somewhere near the service line and set up to volley.

Which is right? They both are! There are going to be times when you can hit on the run because the return is no problem. And there are going to be times when you have to stop and set up or else. Here are three of the or elses:

1) return is a disguised lob that floats over your head as you run by. Since no one can go from forward into reverse without stopping, you've been had;

2) return is an angled passing shot just beyond your reach. Even if you can get your paddle on it you won't manage a decent volley;

3) return is coming right at **you** while you are going right at **it**. The combination of the two forces makes your volley fly well past the baseline and maybe even directly into the screen.

It is one of the paradoxes of paddle that the weaker the serve, the closer the server can get to the net - while the harder the serve, the deeper in the court you'll have to make your approach volley. This is not to say a weak serve is better. A hard serve will probably get lobbed back, not driven. In that case you will be positioned at midcourt for an overhead and not a volley.

Let's approach the approach volley a different way. What you want to do is tailor your style to the style of the returner. If the returner drives well, stop at midcourt. If the returner has a nothing drive, keep coming. If

(continued)

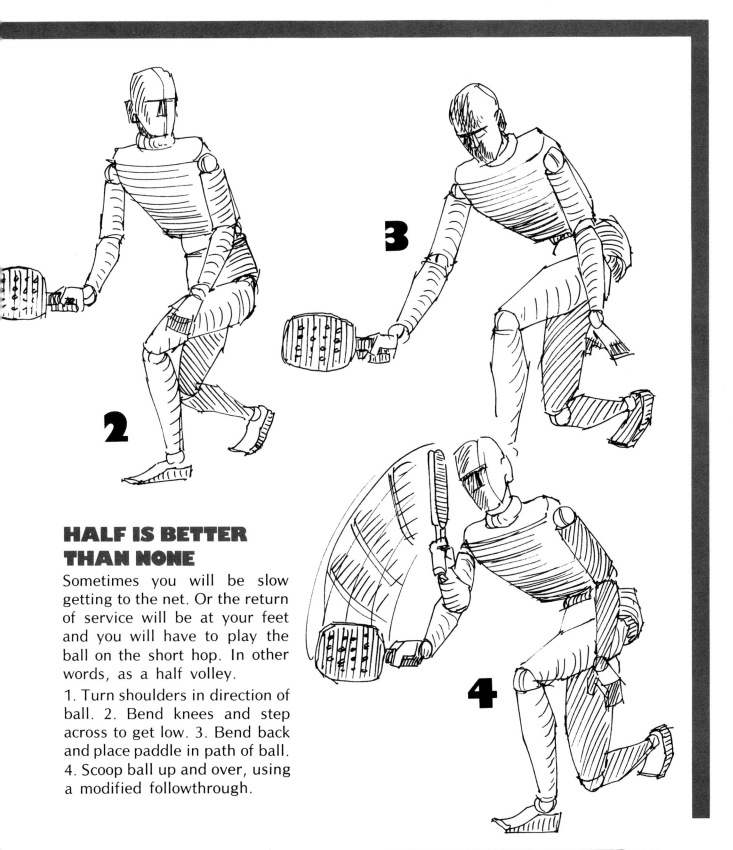

HALF IS BETTER THAN NONE

Sometimes you will be slow getting to the net. Or the return of service will be at your feet and you will have to play the ball on the short hop. In other words, as a half volley.

1. Turn shoulders in direction of ball. 2. Bend knees and step across to get low. 3. Bend back and place paddle in path of ball. 4. Scoop ball up and over, using a modified followthrough.

FOUR-LEGGED FRIEND

1. Set up a chair on the service line and position yourself to hit a first volley. 2. Have partner drive ball at you. Chair forces you to hit forehand volley with no backswing. 3. "No backswing" does not mean "no followthrough." You are about 10 feet from the net and you want your volley to go deep. So hit it.

the returner lobs **everything**, saunter to the net and hit your best overhead.

Whichever style you use, there are some things they have in common. You must have your paddle up in front of you and ready to meet the ball. Not down by your side like a water bucket. You must watch the ball come off the returner's paddle and plan to meet it out in front of you. No wristiness is needed. Keep your forearm, wrist and paddle all in one piece. You must follow the line of your service to the net. Don't go swinging wide to get to the middle of your service box. Anticipate a return right back at you, and that means a backhand volley. If the ball is wide to your forehand side, resist the impulse to take a backswing. Instead reach forward for the ball with your paddle and knock it off while it is still in front of your body.

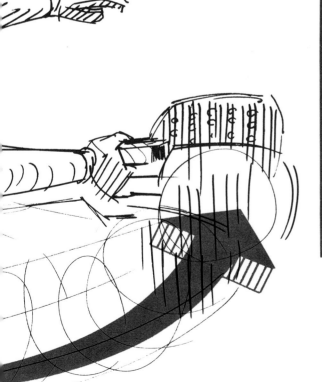

SUMMARY OF VOLLEYING BASICS
1. HOLD TIGHT
2. HUG THE NET
3. STAY ALERT
4. FAVOR THE BACKHAND
5. ATTACK THE BALL
6. FOLLOWTHROUGH, YES - BACKSWING, NO
7. KEEP IT DEEP
8. W — — — T — — B — — —

TROUBLESHOOTING THE VOLLEY

How to use the **TROUBLESHOOTING SECTION.** First, identify the specific problem you are having. Then, relate the NUMBERS in the column opposite your problem to the possible DIAGNOSES listed below. By the process of elimination you will arrive at the cause or causes of your PROBLEM.

Problem	Diagnoses
Volleying into the net	1, 2, 4, 5, 6, 7, 11, 12, 15, 17, 19, 20, 21
Volleying long	1, 3, 9, 10, 11, 19
Volleying wide	1, 10, 11, 20
Popping the ball up	3, 11, 12
Volleying short	2, 3, 5, 11, 12, 15, 17, 21
Lack of power	5, 11, 12, 16, 17
Being passed at net	1, 2, 6, 8, 9, 11, 13, 14, 18
Playing too many half volleys	2, 14, 18
Off-center hits	1, 5, 9, 11, 20

1. Taking too much backswing
2. Standing too far from net
3. Paddle face too open
4. Paddle face too closed
5. Limp wrist, loose grip
6. Paddle head below net
7. Not bending knees
8. Stepping with wrong foot
9. Running into ball
10. Trying for too many winners
11. Not watching ball
12. No followthrough
13. Not zoning laterally
14. Not recovering fast enough
15. Hitting down, not out
16. Not hitting out front of you
17. Weight back, not forward
18. Not concentrating
19. Thinking forehand not backhand
20. Paddle face angled sideways
21. Elbow up in the air

TESTING — 1, 2, 3

Get a friend and some practice balls. You stand at the net and have your friend hit you drives. Object is to volley deep, between service line and baseline. Refinement: have friend call 1, 2, or 3 as he feeds you the ball to designate which part of backcourt you should aim for. Practice volleying from a variety of positions at the net to simulate game action.

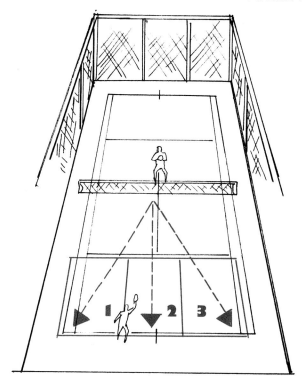

QUIZ

1. The most common volley is (the backhand volley, the drop volley, the lob volley).

2. Good volleyers (aim for the side screens, use lots of topspin, move laterally with the ball).

3. If you volley on the run you risk (being lobbed, underhitting the ball, bumping into your partner).

4. The best aim point for a volley is (the alley, the service box, the backcourt).

5. Volleys should be hit (in preference to overheads, with a firm wrist, to the opponent's forehand).

6. It's good to stand (fairly close to the net, with your paddle just below net level, braced solidly on your heels).

7. The least effective volleying grip is (the Continental, the Eastern, the Western).

8. A good description of the volley is (a slash, a punch, a swing).

9. If you hit a volley from below net level (close your paddle face about 45 degrees, open your paddle face, relax your grip more than usual).

10. It is not important for a volleyer to have (good reflexes, an attacking attitude, picture perfect form).

1. THE REVERSE SHOVEL SHOT OFF THE SCREEN.
Try standing sideways instead. You have more options.

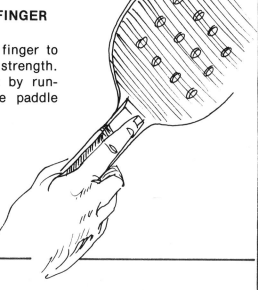

2. THE FOREFINGER FALLACY.
You need this finger to get added grip strength. Don't waste it by running it up the paddle handle.

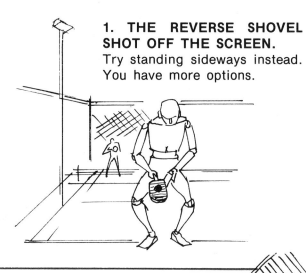

3. WORST NO-NO OF ALL.
Flagging balls that are going to go out turns their errors into their winners!

4. CAUGHT IN THE NET.
Reaching over or touching the net is against the rules. Stay out of their territory.

5. ZERO-PERCENTAGE PLAY.
Driving from five feet behind the baseline against entrenched net players. This is lob time.

6. THE TENNIS TRAP.
Not going to the net behind your serve is like trying to score runs without coming to bat.

LOB

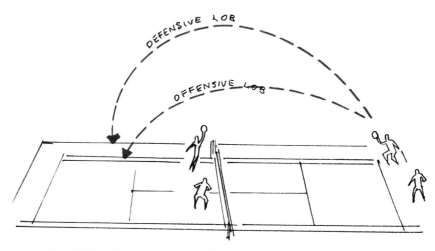

WHAT THE LOB IS

The lob is a two-way shot, offensive or defensive, with the emphasis on the latter. Sometimes a defensive lob is hit so well that it becomes an offensive shot even though its original intent was merely to keep the ball in play. And keeping the ball in play is the lob's basic purpose.

The safest place to aim a lob is at the T formed by the intersection of the service lines in the center of the court. Even if you miss your target by as much as 10 feet, the ball will still land in the court.

Good lobbers get the ball somewhat deeper than midcourt, aiming to make the ball drop closer to the baseline than to the service line. This shot is not an attempt to win points outright, but merely to force the net team to stretch out, back up, and work harder in order to hit their overheads. The theory is that the further back you send them and the more they have to jump and reach for the ball, the likelier it is that they will produce a shallow-bouncing overhead. And that is the kind of shot that you can get offensive with.

Lobs need to have both height and depth, but not too much of either. Avoid the rainmaker, which risks bouncing out of the cage. And avoid the baseline-bouncer; it is an unnecessary risk to take.

Here are specific situations that call for lobs: whenever the ball is volleyed deep and low in your backcourt ... whenever the ball comes off the screen and stays behind the baseline ... whenever a serve can't be taken on your forehand side ... whenever a serve that can be taken on the forehand can't be driven ... whenever you are out of position and need to buy time ... whenever the opponents are tired or have faulty overheads ... whenever the sun is shining in their eyes. Lobbing is a lot like fouling off pitches - it keeps you in the game until you get a ball you like.

Offensive lobbing situations are generally tactical. For example, when playing against a server who tries to get to the net in one quick sprint, a lobbed service return can destroy his game. Against lefty-righty teams, throw up a lob when both their backhands are in the middle.

A good all-around rule of thumb is: when in doubt lob.

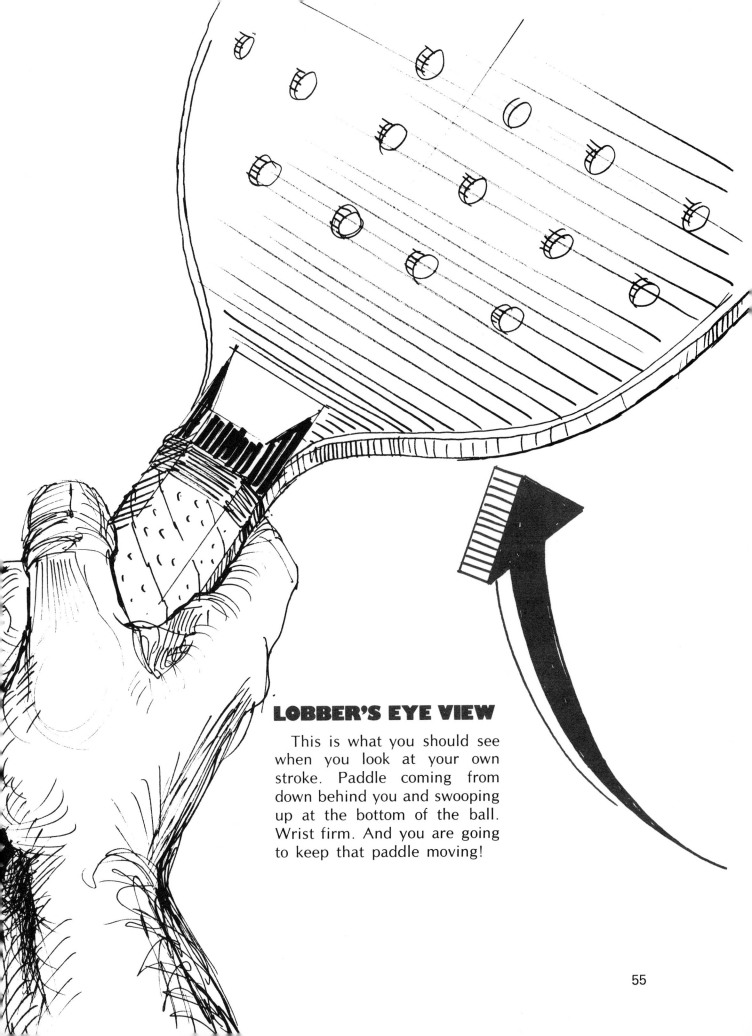

LOBBER'S EYE VIEW

This is what you should see when you look at your own stroke. Paddle coming from down behind you and swooping up at the bottom of the ball. Wrist firm. And you are going to keep that paddle moving!

55

LOB

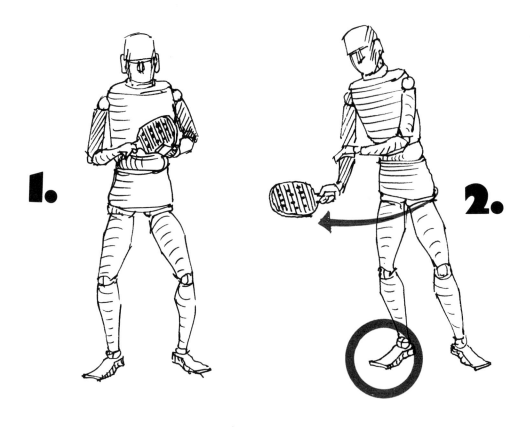

1. READY POSITION
You use the same ready position for the lob as for the drive. In fact, until the ball comes you aren't certain what stroke you are going to hit.

2. THE TURN
Turn your shoulders in the same direction that the ball is coming. Then turn the hips and pick up your back foot. Plant your weight on that foot as you take your backswing.

3. STAY COMPACT
Keep your paddle below the path of the ball. Bend at the knees and the waist. Be sure your elbow is down near your waist, not sticking out away from your body.

4. FLOW INTO THE SHOT
Step toward the ball. Whenever possible you hit the ball while it is still in front of you. Reach under it with your paddle. Your weight is on your forward leg as you make contact. Knees bent, eyes glued to ball. Try for a thigh-high hit.

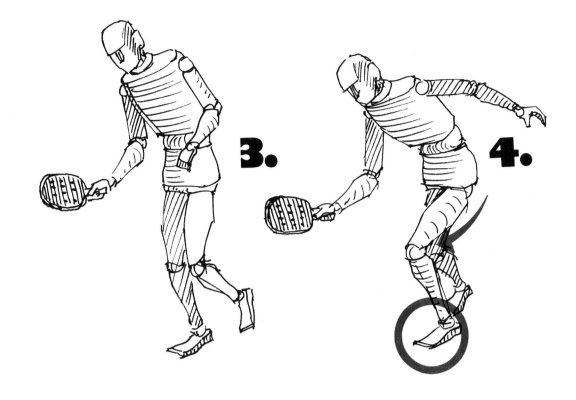

3.

4.

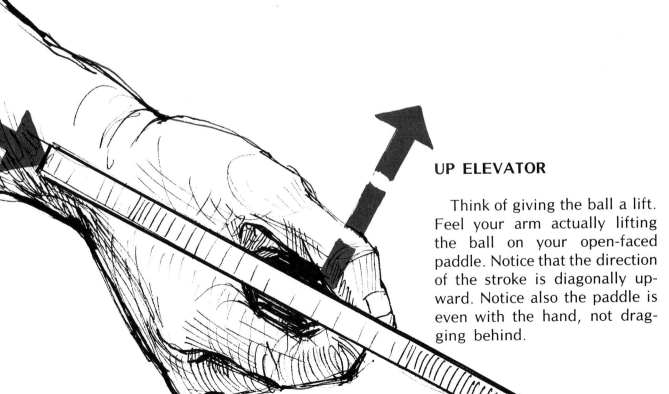

UP ELEVATOR

Think of giving the ball a lift. Feel your arm actually lifting the ball on your open-faced paddle. Notice that the direction of the stroke is diagonally upward. Notice also the paddle is even with the hand, not dragging behind.

STEP RIGHT UP ...

While the ball is coming to you, you are also moving to the ball. The proper cadence is: BOUNCE, STEP, HIT. If your timing is too quick (STEP, BOUNCE, HIT) you will have to rush your swing with erratic results. If your timing is way late (BOUNCE, **NO** STEP, HIT) the ball may get all the way to your back foot before you swing. Or you may just give it a desperation flick as it goes by. Try counting the cadence as the ball comes your way and you will hear for yourself whether you are too slow, too fast or just right.

... AND TOUCH THE SKY

What does a brand new car have in common with a lob stroke? A high finish, of course. Remember that it is the follow-through that determines the direction of the ball. The direction you want is UP, so the paddle has to finish UP. By finishing UP and to your right, the ball will go deep and to the

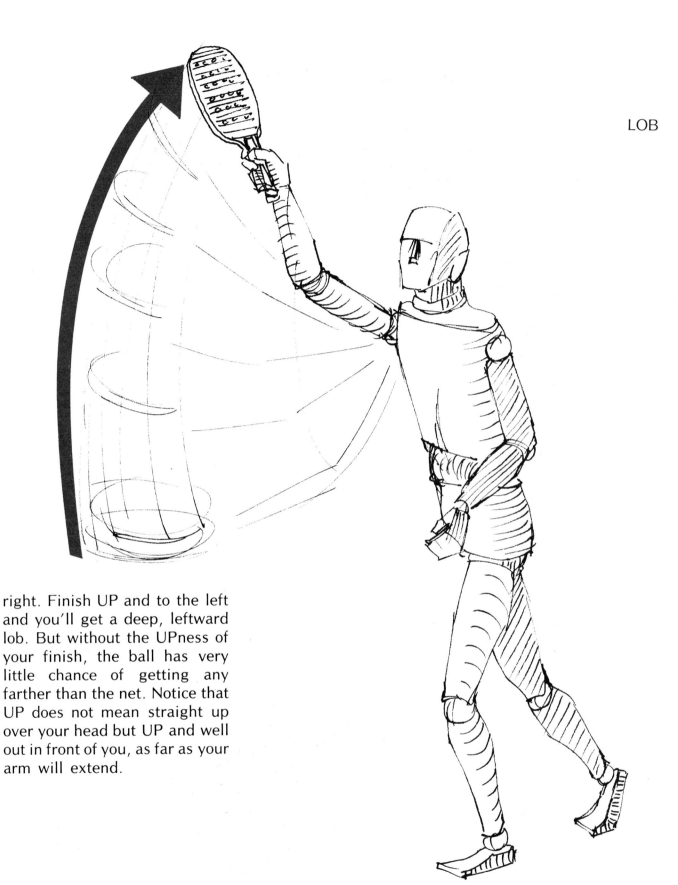

right. Finish UP and to the left and you'll get a deep, leftward lob. But without the UPness of your finish, the ball has very little chance of getting any farther than the net. Notice that UP does not mean straight up over your head but UP and well out in front of you, as far as your arm will extend.

TROUBLESHOOTING THE LOB

How to use the **TROUBLESHOOTING SECTION.** First identify the specific problem you are having. Then relate the NUMBERS in the column opposite your problem to the possible DIAGNOSES below. By the process of elimination you will arrive at the cause or causes of your PROBLEM.

Problem	Diagnoses
Lobs don't clear the net	2, 3, 4, 5, 10, 11, 12, 13
Lobbing too long	1, 3, 9, 10
Lobbing wide	6, 7, 8, 9, 10, 12, 13, 14
Not enough depth	2, 3, 4, 5, 6, 8, 11, 13
Too much height	1, 2, 9
Can't direct ball	4, 7, 8, 9, 10, 12, 14
Hitting late	1, 10, 13
Swing and miss	1, 3, 5, 6, 8, 9, 10

1. Taking too much backswing
2. Paddle face too open
3. Paddle face too closed
4. Limp wrist, loose grip
5. Not bending knees
6. Stepping with wrong foot
7. Standing too close to ball

8. Standing too far from ball
9. Swinging too hard/fast
10. Not watching ball
11. Not enough backswing
12. No followthrough
13. Weight on back foot
14. Paddle face angled sideways

TESTING THE LOB

Take a position behind either alley. Lob 5 balls with your forehand so that they land between the service line and the baseline. Repeat with the backhand. Balls must go high enough to clear the outstretched arm of an imaginary net player. When you can do this 4 out of 5 lobs, narrow the targets to land balls in areas 1, 2 and 3. For further development, get a friend to hit the balls to you and make you run for them.

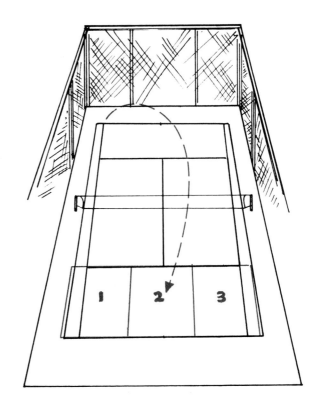

1. The lob is (the ideal return of service, the safest shot to play when in doubt, supposed to land in the alley).

2. The lob requires (a full, high followthrough, an open stance, taking a high backswing).

3. The ideal lob is (very high and very deep, fairly high and fairly deep, reasonably high with no regard for depth).

4. An offensive lob (should chase the net players away from the net, has a higher arc than a defensive lob, often provokes a backhand overhead).

5. Lobs should be hit with (definite underspin, pronounced topspin, no particular attempt to get spin).

6. A good lobber (is one who lobs everything, can drop the ball right on the baseline, makes the net players stretch to hit their overheads).

7. To lob you should hit (with a slightly closed paddle face, with a sharp wrist snap, with a slower motion than a drive).

8. Lobbing on a bright sunny day is (a good tactic, dirty pool, something you do only if they do it to you).

9. If your lob passes the net players (you have won the point, you and your partner should run to the net, go into the I-formation).

10. The usual answer to a lob is (a drop volley, another lob, a crosscourt overhead).

OVERHEADS

WHAT THE OVERHEAD IS ALL ABOUT

The overhead is the offensive answer to a lob, a sort of high volley hit with almost a service motion. Overheads are your best chance to get the ball into the screens, thus forcing your opponents to play defensively.

In tennis the overhead is the ultimate putaway. In paddle it is just part of the jockeying for the point. In tennis you hit the over-head so hard that the shot is usually called a smash. In paddle if you hit it that hard you will find yourself eating the ball!

Forehand overheads are easier to control than backhand overheads, so let the player who can take the ball on his forehand do the hitting.

It is better to keep playing the same defensive player during a rally than to alternate back and forth.

It is better to keep the ball on the defender's backhands than challenge their forehands.

It is better to vary the angle, spin, and speed of the ball than to hit the same shot every time.

Placement is more important than power.

A ball that is dropping as it hits the screen is harder for the defenders to play than one that is rising.

When a lob forces you to back up, it is better to direct your overhead down the middle of the court than to risk an error by trying for an angle.

It is better to call YOURS or MINE on every overhead (even the obvious ones) than to be in doubt about who is going to hit.

On short, weak lobs try to do something extra with the ball. The chance to hit a winner comes too seldom to pass up. End the point if you can.

In a lob-overhead rally of some length, it is not necessary for the overhead hitter to keep coming back to the near-net position. Stay a few feet deeper than partner and cover the entire middle of the court.

Good aim-points: the nick; deep in the side wire; the end panels of the back wire; low in the center panel of the back wire; right at the feet of either defender.

Hitting crosscourt is less likely to result in an error on your part than trying to thread the needle of hitting down the alley.

Don't play yourself to exhaustion by putting your all into every overhead.

YOU'RE THE QUARTERBACK

If you've ever seen a football game you have a fair idea of the mechanics involved in hitting a decent overhead.

Visualize the quarterback. It's third down and you know he's got to pass. He scuttles back from the center, sets up sideways and sticks his forward arm up like a pointer. His throwing arm is cocked behind his head. His forward arm tracks the receiver as he estimates the receiver's speed. He judges when it is time to throw, and with a quick release, he snaps his wrist and permits his throwing arm to flow naturally across his body.

A good overhead follows a similar pattern. You shuffle back sideways to your target, sight the ball over your extended forward arm, cock the paddle behind your head and time the arrival of the ball in the hitting zone. Then at the magic moment, you throw your paddle at the ball with a smart snap of the wrist, and follow through across your body.

There is good logic to each phase of this continuous action.

By turning sideways you make it easier to hit the ball in any direction you choose, with any spin in your repertoire, and with as much power as you feel is called for. If you were to be parallel to the net as you hit, it would be more difficult to control the direction of the ball (it would nearly always go straight) or to add any spin or speed to the stroke. The net-facing overhead will do in a

64

pinch if all you want is to slap the ball softly down the middle. But it stops you from getting any weight into the swing and it is a bad habit to get into.

Turning sideways also makes it quite a bit more comfortable for you to back up to handle those deep lobs. It is so much easier to shuffle crab-fashion than to hop backwards and maintain your balance. Also you may wish to jump up to meet the ball for a little extra something; and this is a hard act to pull off when your weight is on both heels instead of bouncing on your toes.

The extension of the forward arm serves two purposes. As a sighting mechanism it helps you track and time the ball to ensure that you hit it while it is still out in front of you. Then too, it counterbalances the weight of the paddle behind your head. Recall for a moment your service motion: the tossing arm high in front, the hitting arm behind your head. Think of the forward arm in the overhead stroke as a carryover from the forward arm in the service stroke. This will help to smooth out your overhead and make it feel fluid. Not to mention the cosmetically smart look of a stroke hit with graceful form.

The wrist-snap and follow-through complete the action, providing both spin and direction. Again, think of the service: by hitting around the ball you make it hop when it bounces.

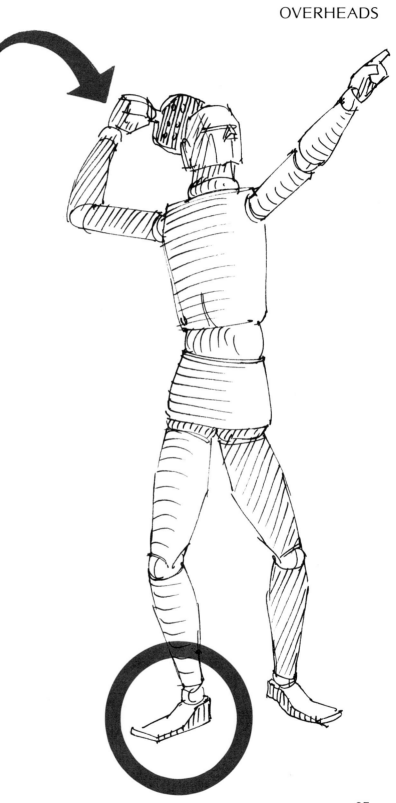

OVERHEADS

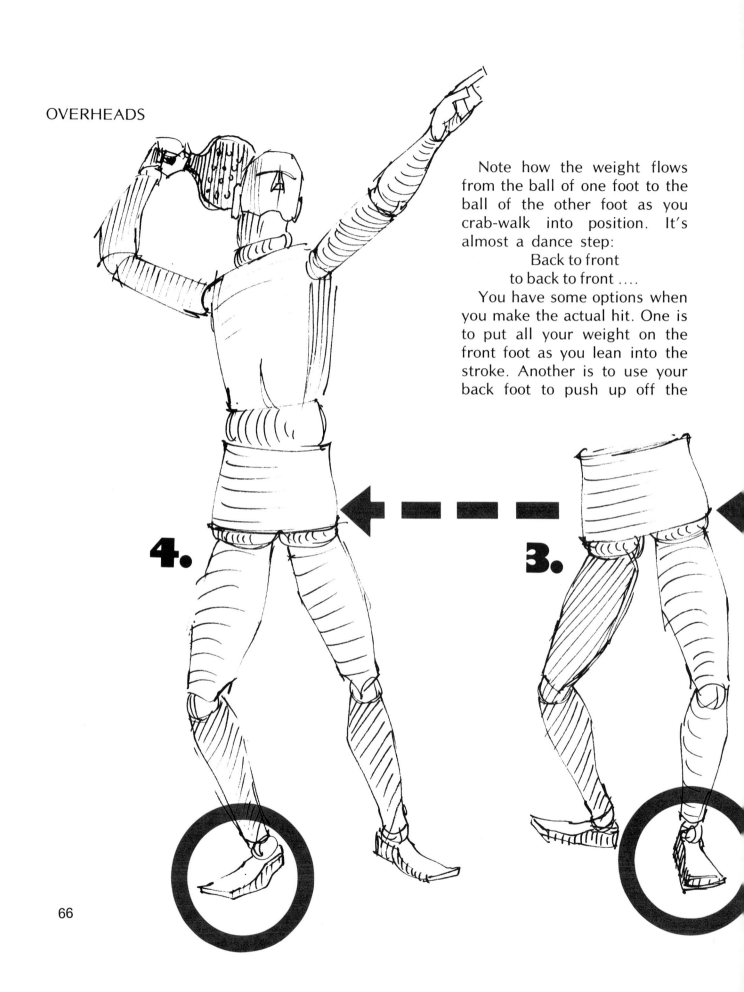

Note how the weight flows from the ball of one foot to the ball of the other foot as you crab-walk into position. It's almost a dance step:
Back to front
to back to front ....
You have some options when you make the actual hit. One is to put all your weight on the front foot as you lean into the stroke. Another is to use your back foot to push up off the

4.

3.

ground. If you do this your legs
will scissor kick in the air and
you will land on your front foot
as you follow through. This
latter technique lets you go up
after the ball and hit down with
extra leverage. The action is
really quite simple and takes
place naturally. You don't have
to force the scissor kick at all -
merely jumping up off the back
foot will cause it to happen.

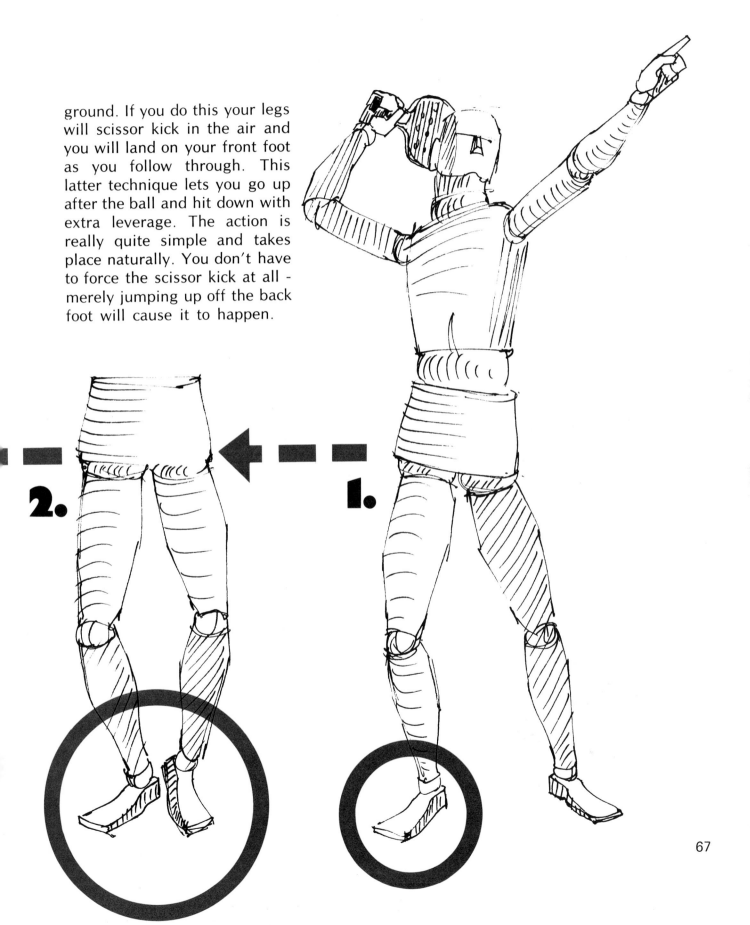

2.

1.

OVERHEADS

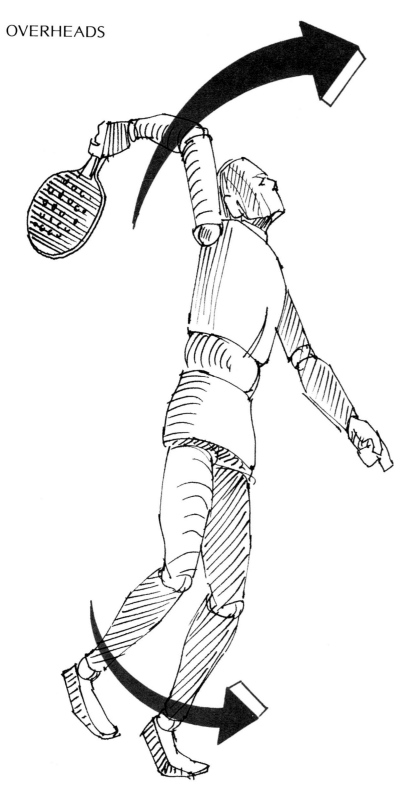

ON THE DOTTED LINE

Be certain to make contact with the ball while it is still in front of your body. You must reach upward and forward both. Letting the ball get even with your head, or worse yet, behind you, will result in a push rather than an overhead.

If you want to hit the ball so it bounces deep in the court and stays low in the screens, keep your wrist frozen and hit through the back of the ball (1) with more forward motion. If you wish to make the ball bounce higher, over the head of the defender and start downward before it hits the screen, snap your wrist and hit (2) with a pronounced downward motion. In the latter case be sure to hit the ball hard enough so that it does not hang in the air short of the screen, thus giving the defender an opportunity to hit a backcourt overhead right back at you.

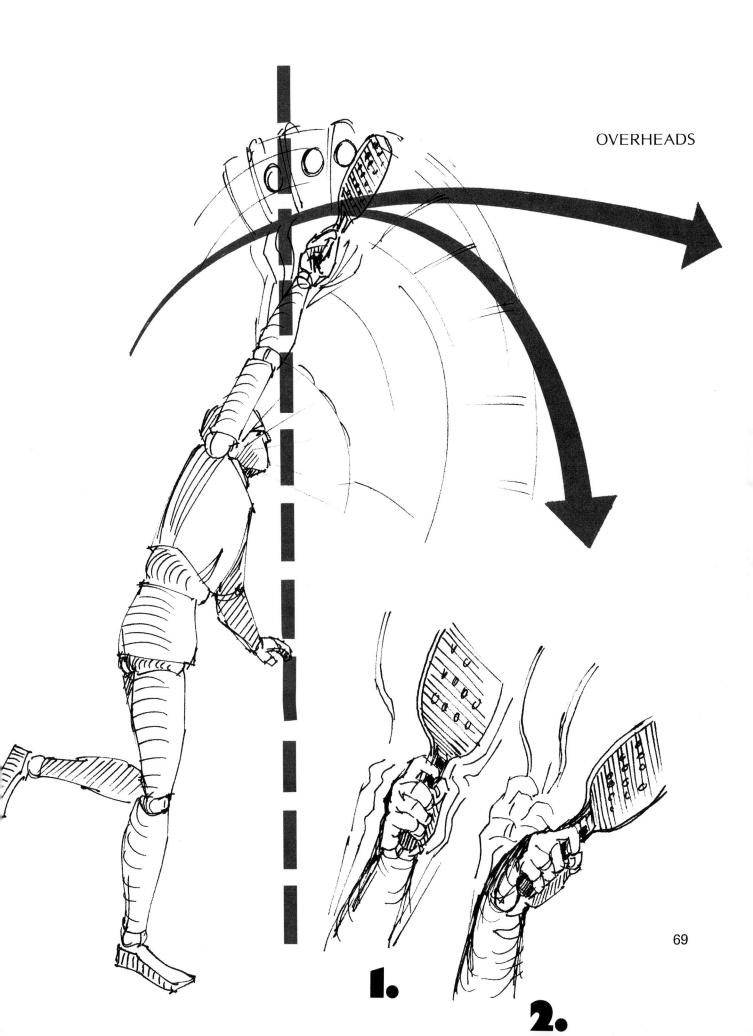

1.

2.

How to use the **TROUBLESHOOT-ING SECTION.** First, identify the specific problem you are having. Then relate the NUMBERS in the column opposite your problem to the possible DIAGNOSES listed below. By the process of elimination you will arrive at the cause or causes of your PROBLEM.

Swing and miss	1, 3, 9, 10
Hitting ball on handle	2, 9, 11, 13
No power	3, 4, 5, 6, 7, 11, 12, 13
Hitting into net	2, 9, 10, 12
Hitting long	1, 9, 10, 12, 13
Poor directional control	1, 2, 4, 7, 8, 9, 10, 11, 12
Hitting too wide	8, 9, 10, 12, 13
Ball pops up	2, 3, 4, 5, 7, 11

1. Swinging too fast/hard
2. Swinging late
3. Letting ball get past you
4. Weight not moving forward
5. Hitting up at bottom of ball
6. Not enough backswing
7. Not enough followthrough

8. Not swinging straight
9. Not watching ball
10. No confidence
11. Letting ball drop too far
12. Not standing sideways to net
13. Not extending hitting arm

TESTING THE OVERHEAD

Stand at the net. Toss up a ball and hit it hard enough, cross-court, to make it bounce into the side wire and carry to the back wire. Do this 5 times. Variation: hit into back wire and make it carry to the side. Vary speed, spin and angle of paddle to achieve different kinds of overheads. For development, have a friend lob the balls back so you are forced to move to hit the overheads.

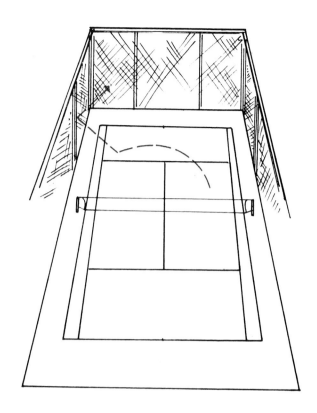

71

BACKHAND

7

WHAT THE BACKHAND IS ALL ABOUT

Of the various shots that can be hit on the backhand side, the drive is least important. Let partner play those shots on his forehand. The court is small enough to encourage that.

Backhand lobs, however, and backhand screen shots are of major importance, as are backhand volleys discussed earlier.

Backhand overheads are emergency shots and should be avoided by having the player who can use his forehand overhead call MINE.

An occasional backhand half-volley will be hit. Half-volleys are defensive shots and can be a sign of poor court position.

Generally, when the ball comes to your backhand side think defense. Be content to keep the ball in play and bide your time.

TURNING ON TO THE BACKHAND

The backhand is a less forgiving stroke than the forehand in that you can hit a respectable forehand drive without getting

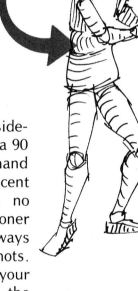

your shoulders completely sideways. But unless you make a 90 degree turn on the backhand side, you can't take a decent backswing. So, no reach, no power, no success. The sooner you get your shoulders sideways the wider your choice of shots. As an aid, make use of your non-hitting hand to pull the paddle head back behind you.

To hit crosscourt, make contact slightly on the far side of the ball. To hit down the line, hit smack on the back of the ball.

Want to experiment with a two-fisted backhand? Be sure to supply power with **both** arms. Otherwise the second hand will just be going along for the ride.

GRIP SESSION

Either the Continental (see Service section) or the Eastern Backhand will work. For the latter, rotate your hand towards the top of the handle. Checkpoints: (1) major knuckle of index finger sits on uppermost plane of handle; (2) thumb makes an angled brace on the plane parallel to the paddle face.

A GOOD FRONT

With the Eastern Backhand you can nail the ball with a perpendicular paddle face while it is still out in front of your leading foot. Keep the arm fairly straight, and lean into the shot. Throw your paddle through the path of the ball pretty much like a frisbee toss, finishing high. (If you hit with the Continental Grip, you will let the ball come back a bit further and make contact closer to where your front foot is.)

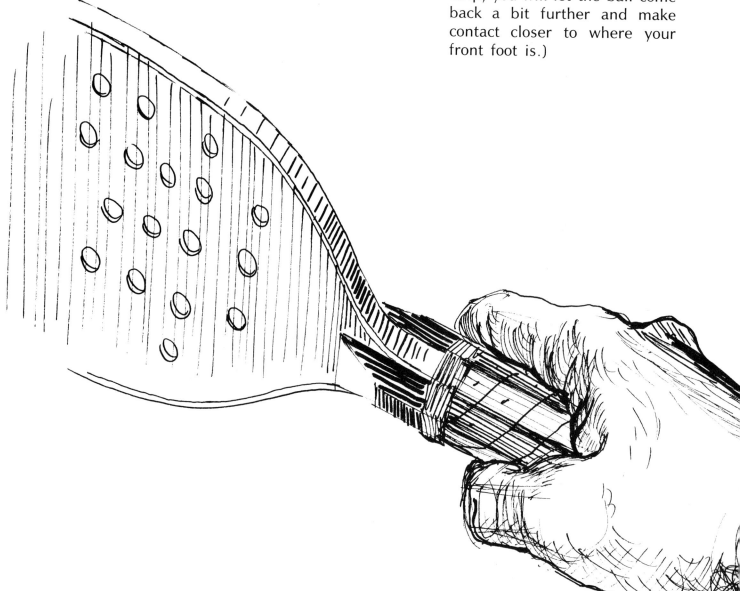

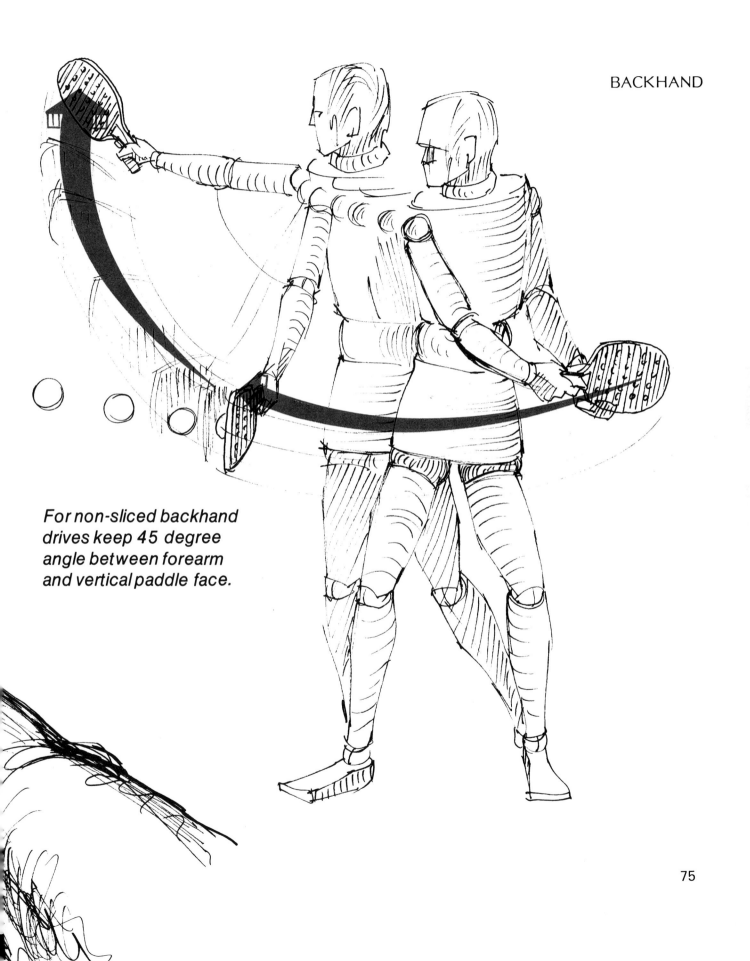

For non-sliced backhand drives keep 45 degree angle between forearm and vertical paddle face.

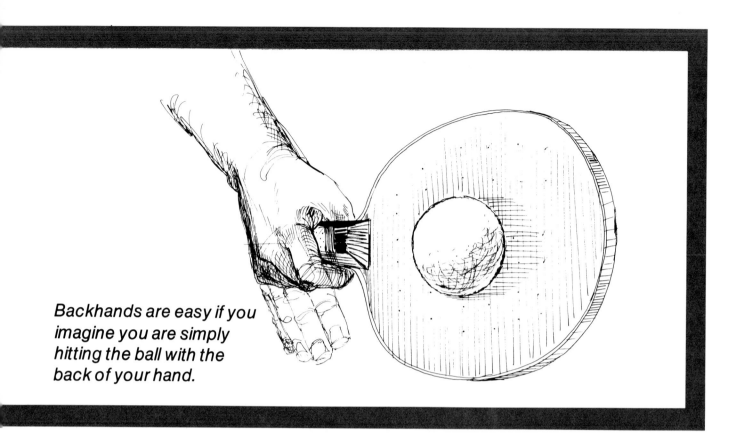

Backhands are easy if you imagine you are simply hitting the ball with the back of your hand.

Game strategy dictates that when you are on defense your backhand will be under more or less constant attack. Therefore, you must develop confidence in all your backhand strokes. Regardless of whether you play the left court or the right court, you will find that your most frequent backhand returns will be lobs.

The mechanics of the backhand lob are different in some respects from the forehand lob. You'll be more secure with a Continental or Eastern Backhand grip. You'll do better to use both hands taking the paddle back. And you'll control your swing better if your hitting arm is quite close to your body on the backswing. Almost wrapped around you in fact. This serves to keep your elbow down and makes it possible to have the paddle lead your swing and not your elbow or wrist.

When the ball comes, step on a slight diagonal toward the hitting spot. Preferably more toward the net than toward the side screen, so that your weight moves forward and not merely sideways. Open the paddle face and swing up from under the ball. And remember to follow through.

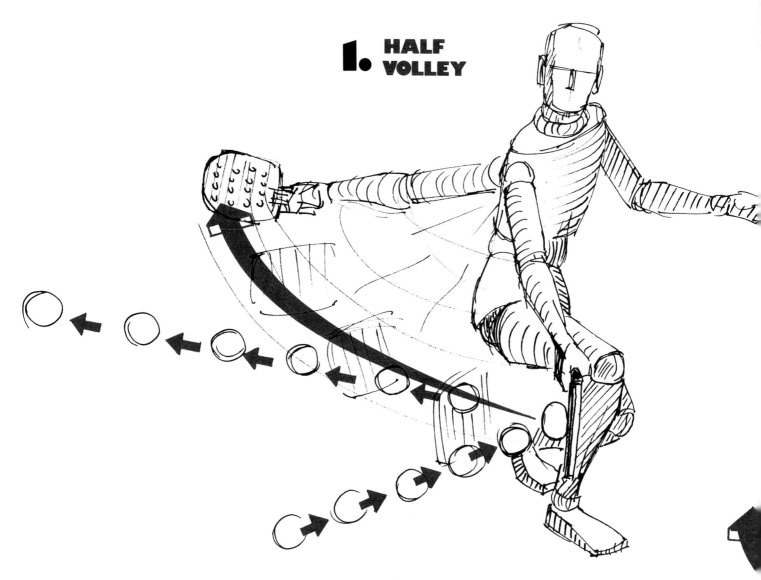

1. HALF VOLLEY

1. HALF VOLLEY

It's all in your knees. Bend, don't stoop. Step to the ball, making contact out in front of you. You must resist the impulse to flinch as the ball bounces into you. Move your paddle into the ball smoothly so that you hit it as soon as possible after it bounces. And keep the paddle moving after the hit.

2. SLICE IT FINE

If drive you must, the sliced backhand is easier to control. Open the paddle face and hit well out in front of you. Contact the ball south of its equator but follow through with a straight-ahead, slightly upward motion. At the finish, paddle should not be below your waist. To get the groove, put your paddle down on the ground and swing into an imaginary ball with your palm facing down.

3. HIGH BOUNCER

The trick here is to keep the plane of your swing level all the way through the shot. Do not snap your wrist or roll your arm because then you will hit down on the ball. Imagine you are tracing a horizon line with your paddle.

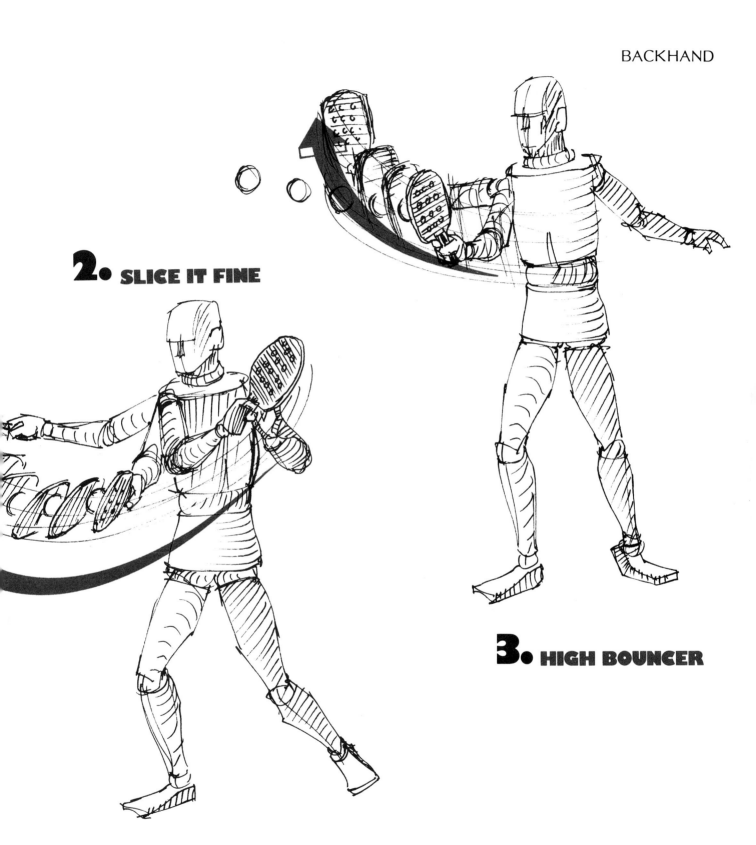

2. SLICE IT FINE

3. HIGH BOUNCER

How to use the **TROUBLESHOOT-ING SECTION.** First identify the specific problem you are having. Then relate the NUMBERS in the column opposite your problem to the possible DIAGNOSES below. By the process of elimination you will arrive at the cause or causes of your PROBLEM.

Hitting into net	1, 2, 3, 4, 7, 8, 10, 12, 13, 14, 15, 18
Hitting long	2, 5, 9, 10, 11
Hitting wide	1, 4, 8, 9, 10, 11, 12, 14, 16, 17
Hitting up	2, 3, 5, 12
Lack of power	1, 2, 3, 4, 5, 7, 8, 11, 12, 14, 16
Off-center hits	2, 4, 7, 9, 10, 11, 14
Swing and miss	1, 4, 9, 10, 11, 15

1. Not turning sideways
2. Elbow sticking up
3. Weight on back foot
4. Late with backswing
5. Paddle face too open
6. Paddle face too closed
7. Limp wrist, loose grip
8. Standing too close to ball
9. Standing too far from ball

10. Swinging too fast/hard
11. Not watching ball
12. No followthrough
13. Hitting down, not through ball
14. Late contact
15. Not bending knees
16. Not hitting out front
17. Hitting too far out front
18. Too high a backswing

TESTING — BACKHAND DRIVE

Position yourself at either A or D. Hit 5 balls over the net so they land between the baseline and the service line. Do this a few times, picking up the pace a little each time. When you get 10 in without a miss, start going for the specific targets 1, 2 and 3. After you become proficient at this, get a friend to feed you the balls so that you have to run to get to them. Work on this drill so that you develop complete confidence in the stroke.

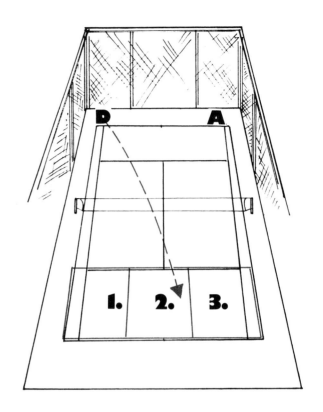

QUIZ

1. The backhand drive is (a powerful offensive weapon, not as important as the backhand lob, a high percentage service return).

2. Backhands can't be hit properly with the (Eastern Forehand, Eastern Backhand, Continental grip).

3. With most backhands you should (hit even with your back foot, lead with your elbow, bend your knees).

4. To hit a backhand lob well, hit (up and out, with slice, a two-fisted shot).

5. It is a good idea to (drive short balls with your backhand, direct backhand overheads crosscourt, run around the backhand).

6. The backhand followthrough (should be below the waist, is not necessary to the shot, should not employ a sharp wrist snap).

7. To hit crosscourt (contact the inside of the ball, contact the far side of the ball, use an open stance).

8. Backhand half volleys (can win by becoming passing shots, are a sign of poor court position, should be permitted to bounce high).

9. The proper angle between forearm and paddle handle is (90 degrees, 180 degrees, 45 degrees).

10. On high bouncing balls it is a good idea to (cover the ball by snapping the wrist, roll the arm over, swing level).

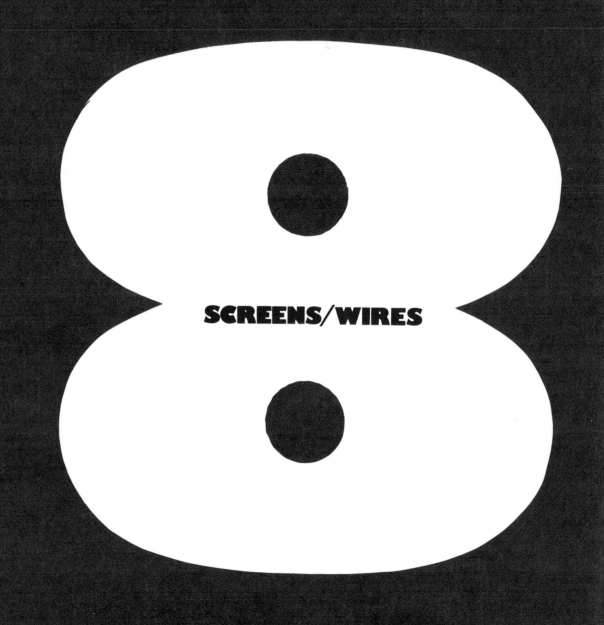

SCREENS/WIRES

WHAT THE SCREENS/WIRES ARE ALL ABOUT

The screens are what platform tennis is all about. Without them we'd have mini-tennis or maxi-ping pong. Think of the screens as your extra partner. Your back-up player who is going to relay the ball to you to make your life easier.

The geometry of the screens is fairly simple: if the ball goes in straight it comes out straight. If it is going upwards as it hits, it is still going upwards when it comes off. An angle going into the screen equals the angle coming off the screen.

The only other thing you need to know is that the screens slow the ball down. They absorb energy just like the bumpers on your car.

What are the practical implications of all this? Well, the geometry lesson tells you that some positions are better to be in than others. In fact, there is a right place to be waiting for every type of rebound. More about that anon.

The knowledge that the ball slows down coming off the screen suggests that you should stand relatively close to the screen to play your shot. And finally, the combined facts (change of direction **PLUS** change of speed) tell you that time is working in your favor. How well you make use of that time determines how well you can play the screens.

If you use the time to glide into position, prepare your feet and your paddle for the stroke, and permit the ball to reach its optimum striking position, you will be a good screen player.

If you waste the time merely watching the ball carom around, then charge to the wire and flail at the ball, you will be a poor screen player.

Final thought: let your eyes direct your actions. The eyes are the fastest elements of your body. They send instant signals to the brain, which in turn instructs your arms and legs where to go and what to do. Trust your eyes. Once they learn a pattern, it becomes part of your memory. In case you have ever wondered why you hear and read the phrase "watch the ball" so often, now you know.

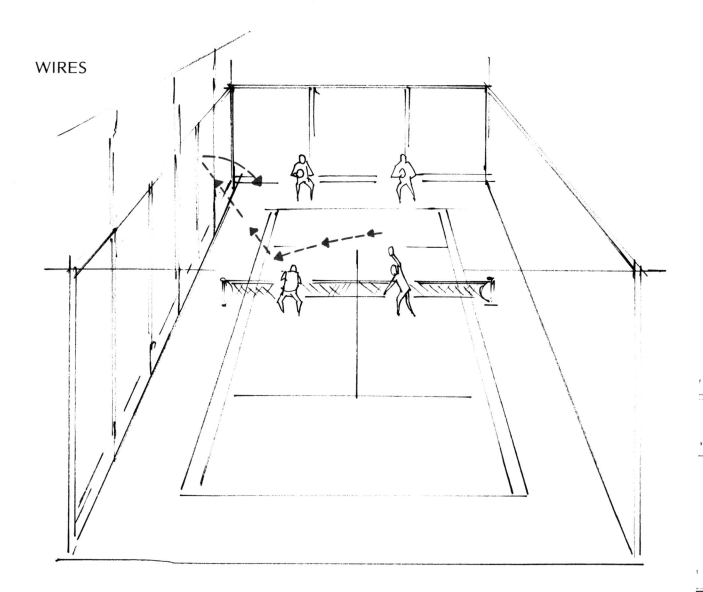

HOW TO BECOME A SCREEN STAR

This is your script for stardom. It progresses from forehand screen shots to backhand screen shots.

For purposes of definition the players are identified as right court players and left court players, and not as forehand players and backhand players. Not only because the former terms are the correct ones, but because both players have to hit off both sides and it comes out confusing to talk about a forehand player's backhand.

GETTING IT WIRED

This is the simplest of all screen shots, **provided** that you do not charge into the ball.

The diagram shows the net player hitting crosscourt and not very deep into the side wire. Any ball that lands on the side wire between the service line and the baseline is more likely to be a one wire shot than a two wire shot.

A side wire forehand is not unlike a groundstroke forehand. The only real difference is that the ball is coming from the side rather than the front, which means it is coming into your body. So the last thing you need

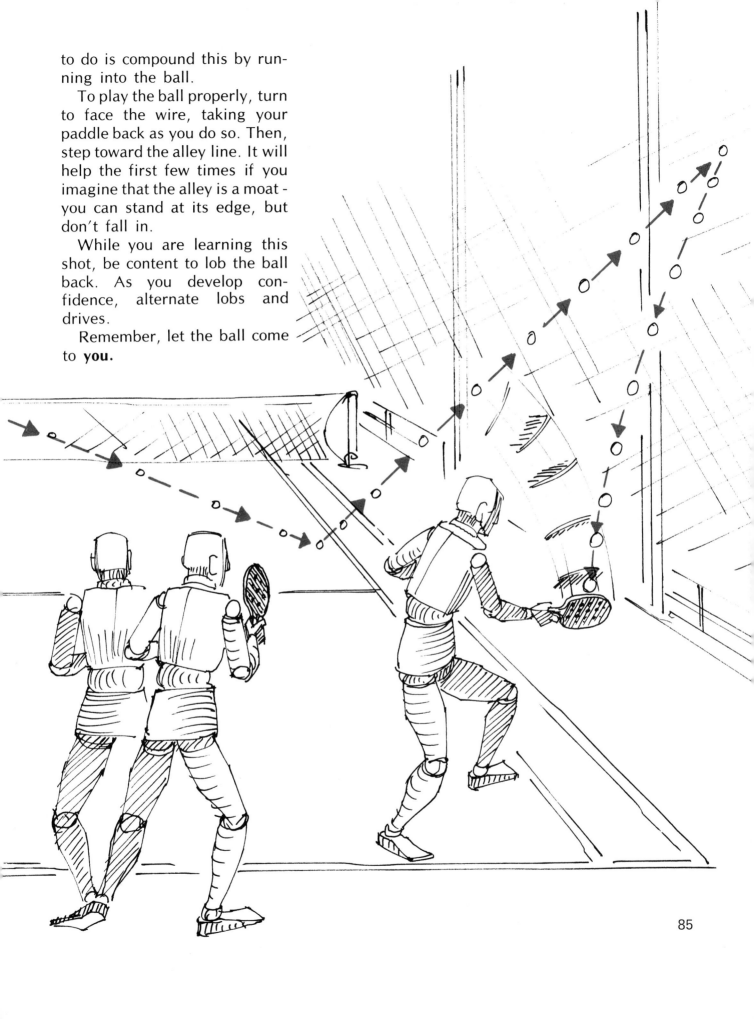

to do is compound this by running into the ball.

To play the ball properly, turn to face the wire, taking your paddle back as you do so. Then, step toward the alley line. It will help the first few times if you imagine that the alley is a moat - you can stand at its edge, but don't fall in.

While you are learning this shot, be content to lob the ball back. As you develop confidence, alternate lobs and drives.

Remember, let the ball come to **you.**

HIGH WIRE ACT

When the ball comes off the wire over your head and you dare not let it go past you, reach up and block the ball. Hit upward or straight through the back of the ball rather than downward. Remember, when you are deep in the court you should play defensively. Don't risk netting the ball by getting aggressive from this far back.

DRIVING FOR FUN AND PROFIT

Teeing off on a side wire shot with your forehand drive is very satisfying and quite easy. It is not necessarily the best shot from a tactical point of view, but if you have a good drive and can get fairly close to the net player, take a whack at it. Be sure to hit the ball while it is still out in front of you, at about waist height. Always pick out a target (the alley, the net player, the middle) in advance; don't just hit aimlessly.

POSITION IS EVERYTHING

The diagrams below and on the next pages show the typical side-to-back wire shot.

Net player has hit crosscourt, and your internal radar system computes that this cannot be treated as a one-wire shot.

As ball hits deck, take your paddle back behind you and turn toward the side wire. Back up with short steps till you are about two feet from the back wire and about ten feet from the side wire. This is a good position to handle a medium speed ball, assuming properly-tensioned wires.

You have plenty of time to drift smoothly into this position as long as you start with the

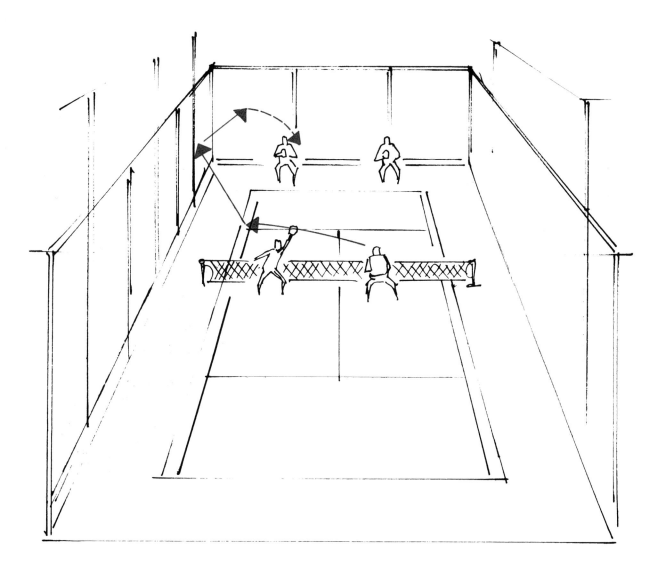

WIRES

bounce of the ball. The wire will slow the ball down and deliver it to where you are waiting. If you permit the ball to get past you before you start moving, you're in trouble.

Resist the impulse to reach up for the ball. Let gravity be your buddy.

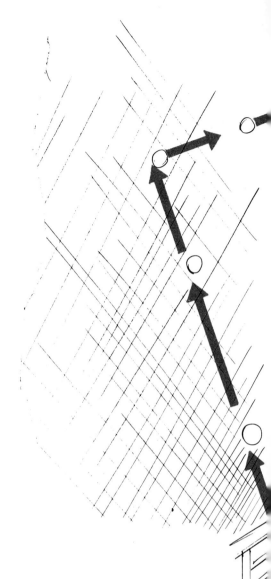

FOLLOW THE BOUNCING BALL

An alternative way to play the left court corner is to follow the ball around the corner with your entire body. As ball hits side wire you take the paddle back for a **forehand** lob. Then you turn, staying under and behind the ball, waiting for it to drop.

This is not the preferred nor most common technique, but some players find that it is the only way that they can cope with side-to-back shots in the left corner.

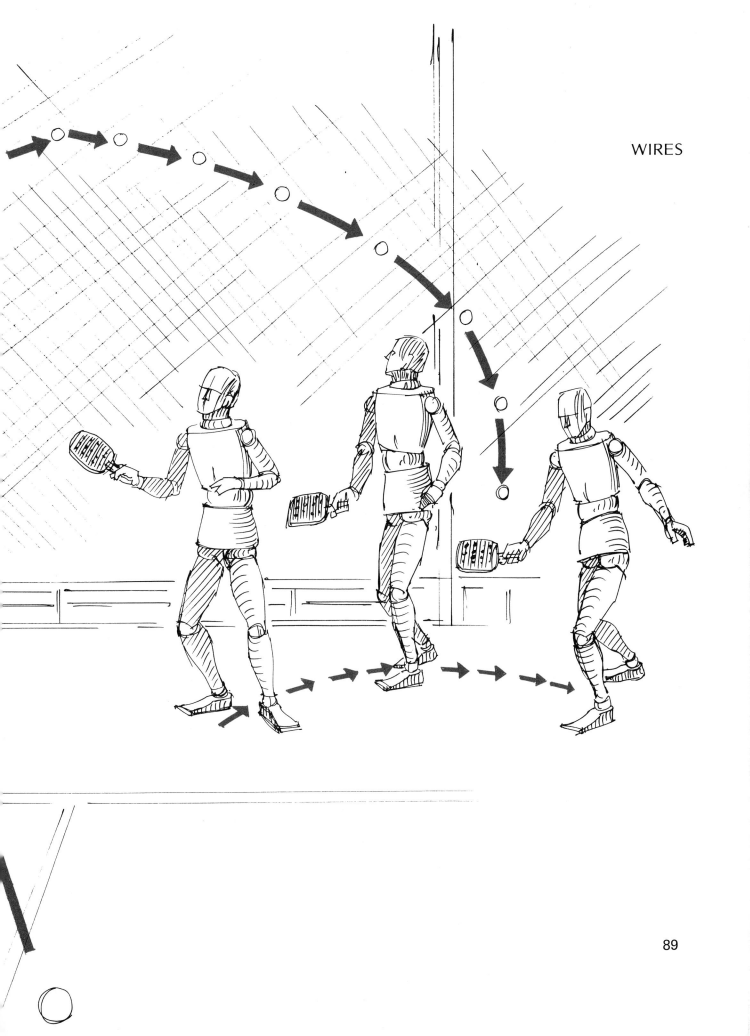

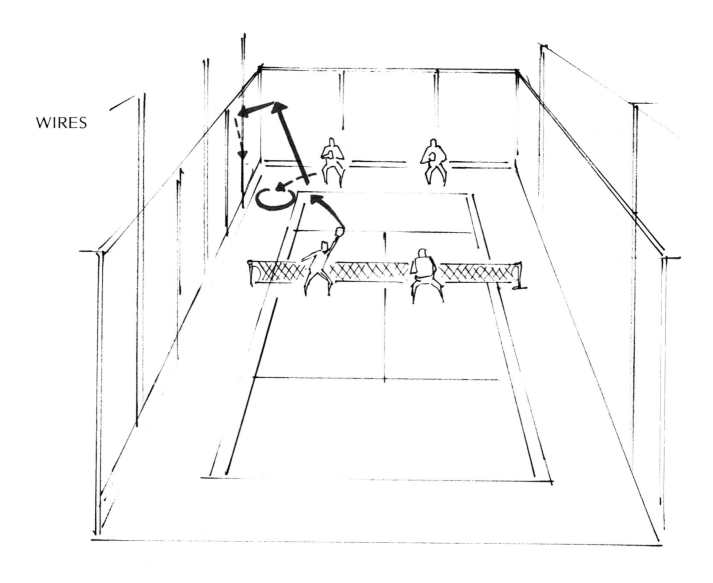

WIRES

MOVING IN THE BEST CIRCLES

This diagram depicts what happens when the overhead is aimed to hit the back screen first and then carom into the side screen.

These caroms are decidely less predictable than side-to-back ricochets. Sometimes the ball does not have enough angle on it to make it carry to the side screen. And in some cases the ball will come out almost parallel to the side screen.

Whatever, when you see the ball pass over your head, push off on your weight-bearing foot and head for the invisible circle about two feet in front of the baseline and just wide of the alley. Wait there for the ball to come to you.

Many beginners lean away from the ball as it passes. This puts their body weight in the wrong direction and usually prevents them from catching up with the ball. Don't lean away from the screen.

As always, get your paddle ready as you start to move with the flight of the ball.

WIRES

This is the one forehand shot played by the left court player. As the ball comes down the middle, turn just as you would for a forehand drive off the deck, taking the paddle back and calling MINE. Watch the ball into and out of the screen. Be patient.

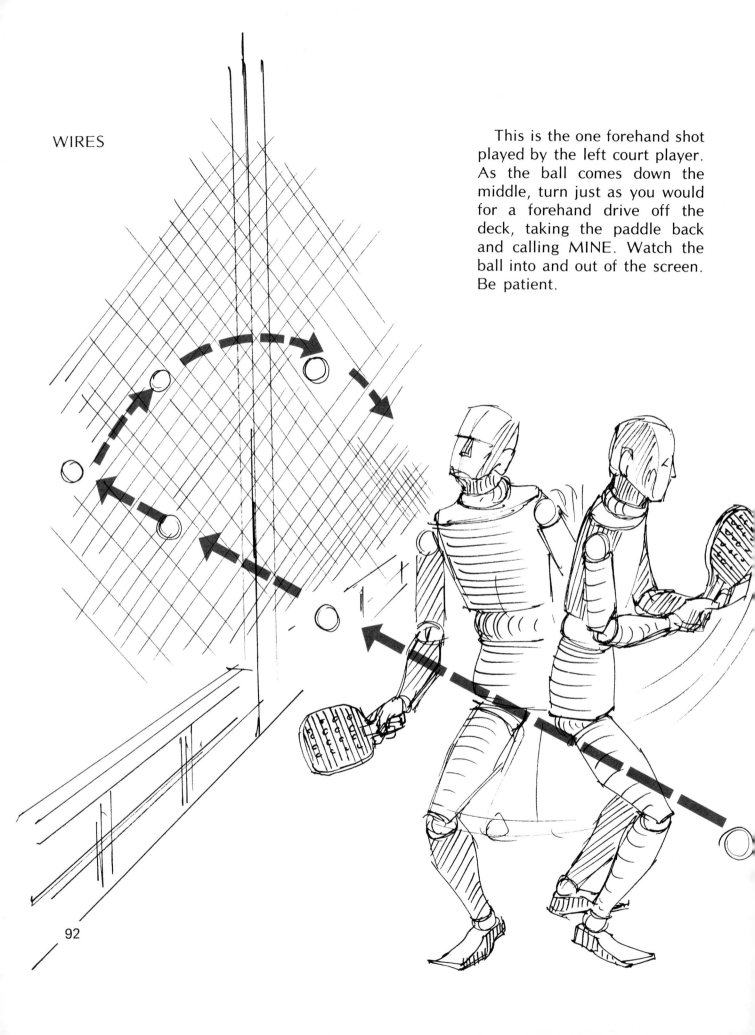

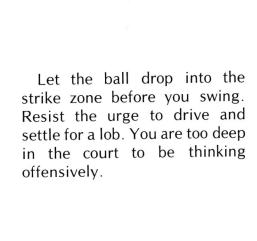

Let the ball drop into the strike zone before you swing. Resist the urge to drive and settle for a lob. You are too deep in the court to be thinking offensively.

FAIR PLAY

Calling YOURS, MINE, HIT, etc. to your partner when the ball is on your side of the net.

Taking an unorthodox position on the court, e.g. receiver standing close to the service line to handle a short ball.

Hitting the ball hard at the woman in a mixed doubles match, when winning matters.

Taking practice serves OR asking for first one in, in a casual match.

Calling all the shots that land on your side of the net.

Asking for a let when there is reasonable cause.

Asking your opponent's opinion on a bounce that caught you unsighted.

Calling the close ones in favor of the opponents.

Admitting your own carries, double hits, not ups, and leaning over or touching the net.

NOT FAIR PLAY

Calling HIT when the ball is on their side of the net in an attempt to make them play an out ball.

Dancing around and waving your arms when the server is going into his motion in an attempt to distract him.

Hitting the ball hard at inexperienced women players in a social match of no consequence.

Taking practice serves AND THEN saying first one in as if it was your right to have both.

Calling all your own shots that land on their side of the net.

Asking for a let when you haven't really got a leg to stand on.

Asking your opponent's opinion and then disregarding it, looking for a free let.

Calling the close ones in your own favor.

Applying the double standard.

THE LOWDOWN ON SCREEN PLAY

It is relatively easy to return balls that come off the screens high with a nice arc to them. But what about softly hit overheads that hug the wire all the way down? The secret is to get down yourself. Very low down. Do a deep knee bend of sorts. Keep your feet fairly close together. The object is to get your body, as well as your arm and paddle, well under the ball.

This lowdown technique applies to both forehands and backhands. And so does the full followthrough. In this position it is hard to get any forward body motion into the shot, so you will have to do a little extra with your arm.

95

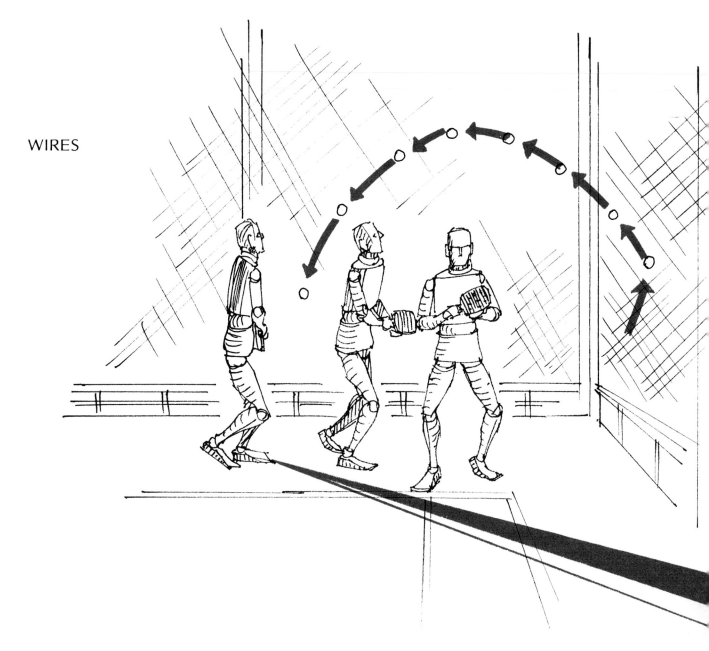

U-TURN PERMITTED

Getting into a good position for side-to-back wire shots on the backhand is a little like making a U-turn in reverse. As soon as you see you're in for a two-wire shot, start backing away, giving the ball room to do its caroming act. Note that although the ball is bounding away from you at first, after it hits the wires it is coming back. Unless you move clear, it will bounce right into you.

The move should be as graceful and continuous as a dance step. Anticipate that the ball will come out about 10 feet or so from the wide wire. You can make adjustments according to the many variables. If the ball is hit very hard, it will come out more than that. Other things that determine the ball's action include the temperature, the humidity, any spin on the ball, and a variety of both obvious and subtle effects, such as the tension of the screens, and even the brand of the ball you are using.

BREAD AND BUTTER BASICS

The body is loose and relaxed. Flexed not tense. Bent at the waist as well as the knees.

The weight moves into the shot on the forward foot. Not by swinging the back foot around.

Contact is made at the most comfortable height - the same as if you were hitting a groundstroke. No rushing or reaching to pick the ball off while it is still over your head.

The followthrough is upward and forward.

During the entire sequence your eyes should stay with the ball. This will clue you in on any irregular caroms. Good tip: keep your eyes aimed at the point of contact between paddle and ball even after you have actually hit it. If you raise your eyes to follow the flight of the ball too soon, you risk muffing the shot.

WIRES

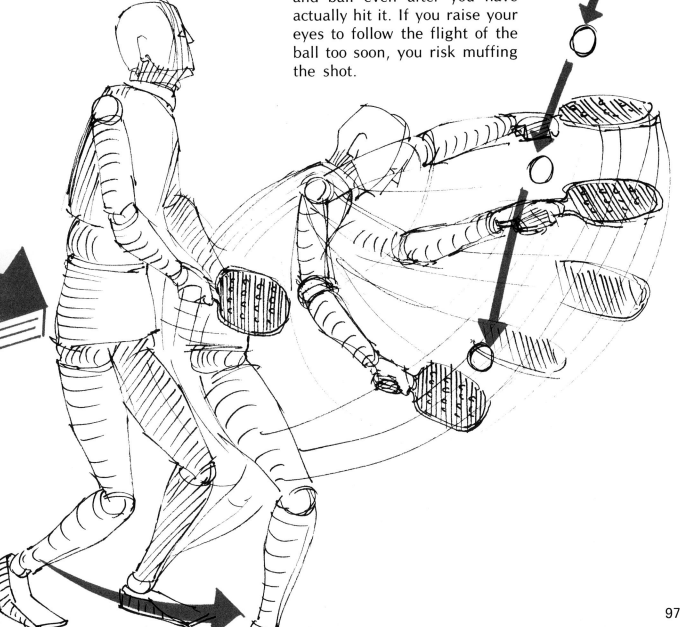

97

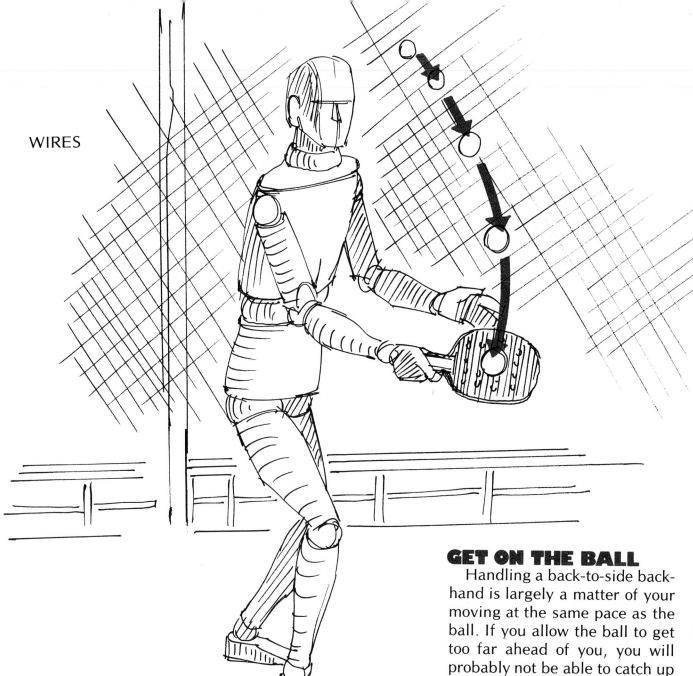

WIRES

GET ON THE BALL

Handling a back-to-side back-hand is largely a matter of your moving at the same pace as the ball. If you allow the ball to get too far ahead of you, you will probably not be able to catch up with it. Try counting a cadence of four:

ONE (ball bounces on deck).
TWO (ball hits back screen).
THREE (ball hits side screen).
FOUR (you hit the ball).

At the first count you should get your paddle back. At the second count you should head for the invisible circle. At the third count you should be under the ball, or no more than a foot behind it. When this shot is missed, it is usually missed by inches, because the player got a late start running out under the ball.

THE UNAVOIDABLE BACKHAND

Virtually all soft overheads hit down the middle will be aimed at the right court defender's backhand. To handle these shots, turn sideways, taking the paddle back, as the ball passes by. Then wait for the ball to come past you going in the opposite direction. Stand fairly close to the back screen and swing slowly under the ball. Lob and live. Drive and die.

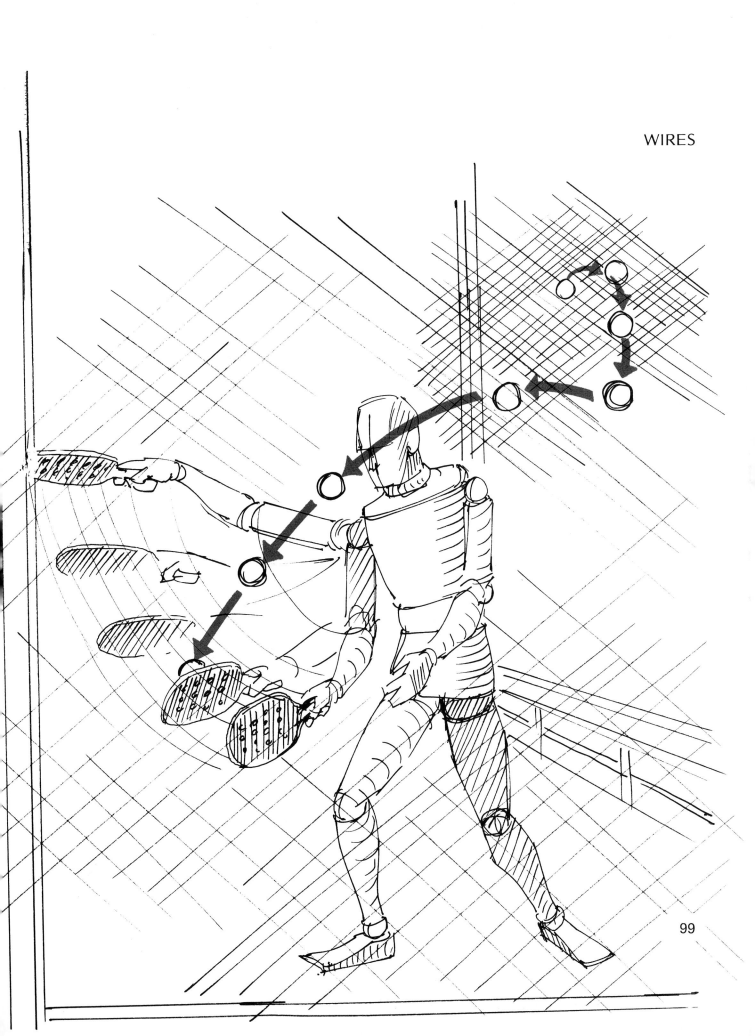

How to use the **TROUBLESHOOTING SECTION.** First identify the specific problem you are having. Then relate the NUMBERS in the column opposite your problem to the possible DIAGNOSES below. By the process of elimination you will arrive at the cause or causes of your PROBLEM.

Problem	Diagnoses
Can't time the ball	1, 2, 3, 5, 6, 13, 14, 15
Swing and miss	1, 2, 3, 4, 5, 6, 9, 11, 13, 15
Hitting/lobbing long	2, 7
Lobbing short	6, 8, 13, 15
Off-center contact	2, 5, 6, 7, 10
Can't control direction of ball	2, 6, 8, 9, 10, 14, 15
Trouble with low balls	1, 3, 5, 7, 9, 11, 12, 14, 15
Driving ball into net	2, 7, 10, 11

1. Too slow/late with backswing
2. Too fast/hard a swing
3. Late getting into position
4. Rushing into the ball
5. Not watching ball
6. Not waiting for ball to drop
7. Paddle face not open
8. No/not enough followthrough

9. Poor court position
10. Too wristy
11. High backswing/hitting down
12. Not bending knees enough
13. Standing flatfooted
14. Too far from screen
15. Not facing sideways

SCREENTESTING

Get a friend who can hit the ball into the screen and move you around. Do this drill without regard for whether you hit or miss the ball at first. The object is to get you into a rhythm. First, attempt 3 forehands off the side, then 3 forehands side to back and finally 3 forehands back to side. A sequence of 12 shots. Now that you have the rhythm, hit for effect. Try to clear the net. When your percentage gets better than 50-50, try to lob the ball into the backcourt. Finally, do a similar drill hitting with your backhand.

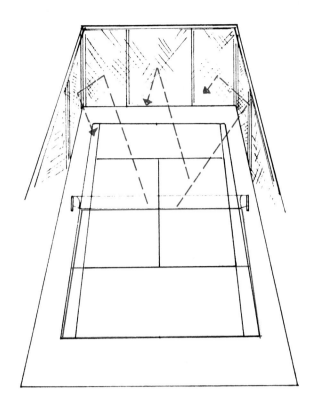

QUIZ

1. When a ball hits the screen (it picks up speed, it is deflected at a 45° angle, it may or may not carom into another screen).

2. It is **not** a good idea to (get your paddle ready as soon as possible, let the ball drop into the best hitting zone, charge at the ball).

3. Most wire shots should be (lobs, drives, volleys).

4. The left court player (should expect to play most of the wire shots, defers all forehands to his partner, rarely gets a chance to hit a backhand).

5. The right court player (must not permit serves to reach the screens, plays a lot of backhands off the back wire, is usually team captain).

6. Skillful wire play does **not** require (waiting for the ball, moving into position as soon as

you can, using controlled top-spin).

7. The invisible circle is (in the alley, wide of the alley, behind the alley).

8. It is relatively easy to return a ball that (comes off the wire high, hugs the wire all the way down, bounces off the top railing).

9. To avoid having to play very difficult wire shots it is permissible to (ask for a let before you take a swing, ricochet the ball directly back into the wire, intercept the ball before it gets to the wire).

10. How the ball comes off the screen is **not** influenced by (speed, spin, make of ball, wetness of court, air temperature, receiver's court position, angle of overhead, screen tension).

QUIZ ANSWERS

SERVE

1. Speed
2. Serve right at the receiver and jam him
3. Up and through
4. The Continental
5. Try serving the ball harder
6. Flat
7. Knee flexion
8. Paddle action
9. Aces are uncommon
10. On its way down

SCREENS

1. It may or may not carom into another screen
2. Charge at the ball
3. Lobs
4. Should expect to play most of wire shots
5. Plays a lot of backhands off the back wire
6. Using controlled topspin
7. Wide of the alley
8. Comes off the wire high
9. Intercept the ball before it gets to the wire
10. Receiver's court position

BACKHAND

1. Not as important as the backhand lob
2. Eastern Forehand
3. Bend your knees
4. Up and out
5. Run around the backhand
6. Should not employ a sharp wrist snap
7. Contact the far side of the ball
8. Are a sign of poor court position
9. 45 degrees
10. Swing level

LOB

1. The safest shot to play when in doubt
2. A full, high followthrough
3. Fairly high and fairly deep
4. Should chase the net players away from the net
5. No particular attempt to get spin
6. Makes the net players stretch to hit their overheads
7. With a slower motion than a drive
8. A good tactic
9. You and your partner should run to the net
10. A crosscourt overhead

FOREHAND

1. Essential for a strong game
2. Laid back
3. Most effective to obtain top
4. By a couple of inches
5. Is merely an option
6. Take a roundhouse backswing
7. Drive shallow volleys
8. The defensive team
9. Shoulder high or even higher
10. Poor directional control

VOLLEY

1. The backhand volley
2. Move laterally with the ball
3. Being lobbed
4. The backcourt
5. With a firm wrist
6. Fairly close to the net
7. The Eastern
8. A punch
9. Open your paddle face
10. Picture perfect form

OVERHEAD

1. A placement
2. Toward the corners or the middle
3. Taken as forehands
4. Bounce the ball out of the enclosure
5. Shuffle sideways
6. You still have a chance to play the ball
7. Hit the net on your followthrough
8. The player in the left court
9. A serve
10. To sight the ball in flight

STRATA-GEMS

STRATA-GEMS

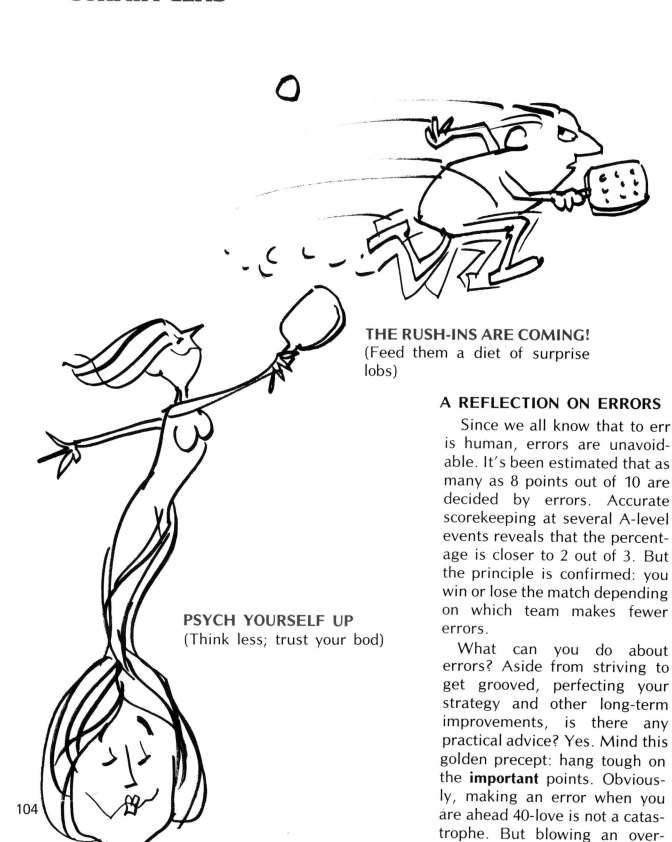

THE RUSH-INS ARE COMING!
(Feed them a diet of surprise lobs)

PSYCH YOURSELF UP
(Think less; trust your bod)

A REFLECTION ON ERRORS

Since we all know that to err is human, errors are unavoidable. It's been estimated that as many as 8 points out of 10 are decided by errors. Accurate scorekeeping at several A-level events reveals that the percentage is closer to 2 out of 3. But the principle is confirmed: you win or lose the match depending on which team makes fewer errors.

What can you do about errors? Aside from striving to get grooved, perfecting your strategy and other long-term improvements, is there any practical advice? Yes. Mind this golden precept: hang tough on the **important** points. Obviously, making an error when you are ahead 40-love is not a catastrophe. But blowing an overhead when the score is ad out - that hurts.

104

POACHED EGG ON FACE
(Don't steal your partner's shot unless you've got a better one)

LEFT IS RIGHT
(Lefties belong in the right court at the net. So switch!)

To paraphrase the old saying, all points are created equal but some are more equal than others. You can get a variety of opinions about which are the most important points, but the arguments can be fairly far out. So to keep it simple, try this formula: 1) the most important point, obviously, is the game point; 2) the next most important point is the one that sets the opponents up with a game point.

In scoring terms this means that ad out and ad in are the super biggies. And the next most meaningful moments come at deuce or 30-all.

If you could arrange to make all your errors on points other than these, clear off your mantelpiece. Make room for the trophies!

105

MORE STRATA-GEMS

Many teams make the mistake of thinking they have the game won when they are ahead 40-love. Wrong! The scoring system is insidiously clever. Leading 40-love is like having a man on third base; he's not a run until he crosses the plate. And it's not a game until you get that fourth point. When you are ahead 40-love, you are in danger. If you let up and lose, it will affect your outlook and your concentration. You may lose the next game out of disappointment. So try this mental trick: pretend you're losing 40-love. It will force you to play carefully, and careful play is the key to winning.

If there is anything worse than losing a 40-love game it is losing when you have 5 games in the bank and the opponents have 2 or less. That kind of disaster cuts two ways: your team feels discouraged - the other team feels elated. And the problem was simply that you were thinking about the score and not about the play. There's that man left on third base all over again.

A rather different situation is losing a match after winning the first set. An analysis of 44 national championship matches that went 3 sets reveals that 20 of them were won by the team that lost the first set. Experienced players do not concede

matches, to themselves or their opponents, on the basis of the first set. And neither should you. Strange as it may sound, some players prefer to lose the first set because they like the challenge of coming from behind. And some players take forever to get warmed up. But then they get hot as pistols. The danger of winning the first set 6-0 is that a team may become

SHALLOW THINKING
(Make them eat their mistakes.
Don't temporize on short balls)

overconfident or contemptuous
of their opponents. As a result
they relax their concentration,
their game falls apart, and down
the tube they go.

Ahead or behind, play each
point - each shot, as if it was the
most important point in the
match, as if you had to win it to
stay alive.

That is what competitive instinct is all about.

GUT INSTINCT
(Make the weaker volleyer do all
the volleying)

STILL MORE STRATA-GEMS

CHEWS UP SIDES

(Hold your tongue and hold the partnership together)

FORMING A PARTNERSHIP

Among the desirable qualities of a partner probably none is more important than availability. So the chances are pretty good that as you are putting your game together your first partner is liable to be a friend, fellow beginner, or a person who plays at the same courts that you do. Keep your options open. One or the other of you will outgrow the partnership before too long. Size up the other players at your level. Make mental notes about who seems to be improving and who has the kind of game you admire. Here are some of the general and specific things you should look for:

1. Willingness to practice and play **regularly.**
2. Agreement on who plays which half of the court.
3. Complementary skills.
4. A healthy respect for each other's ability.
5. A healthy respect for each other as a person.
6. An orientation toward teamwork rather than individual or personal performance.
7. A sense of humor, to cope with the bad days.
8. The power to read each other's mind.

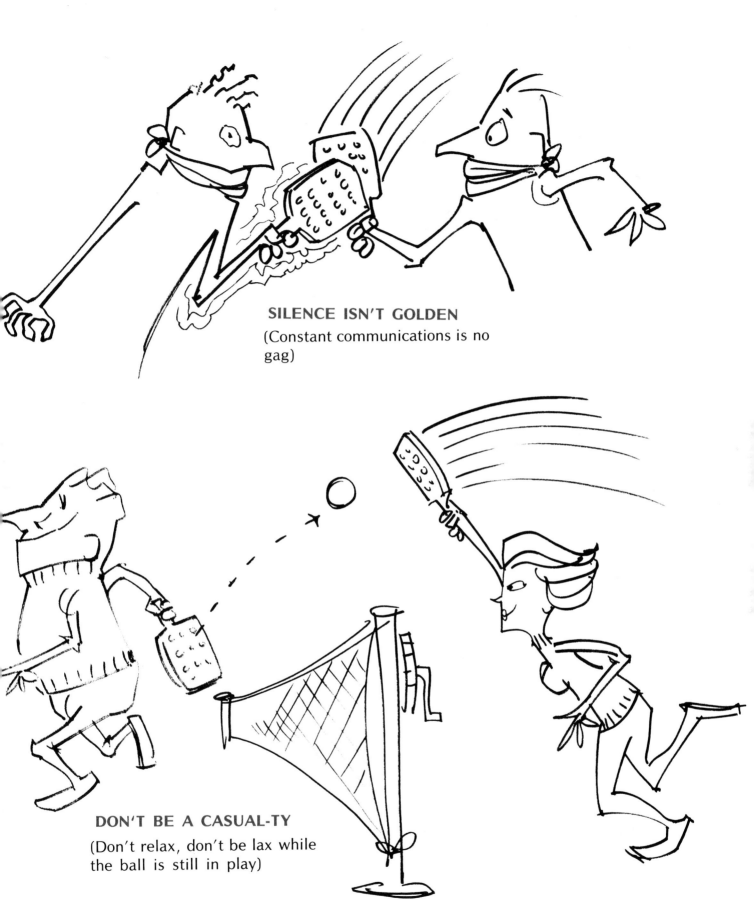

SILENCE ISN'T GOLDEN
(Constant communications is no gag)

DON'T BE A CASUAL-TY
(Don't relax, don't be lax while the ball is still in play)

ODDS &

CLOTHING

Informal. That's the only word for it. Some players are into funk, others favor fashion. It's whatever turns you on. Just be sure you wear tennis shoes or sneaks. Good tip: in cold weather dress in layers so you can peel as you perspire.

EQUIPMENT

Paddles run from about $10 up to $40. Don't get stuck with a piece of paddleball or racquetball equipment by mistake. Specify "for **platform** tennis." Dry off your paddle if you play in the rain. Water's no good for wood.

Balls cost about a buck. New ones bounce better and are easier to see than old ones. They last a set or a week depending on how skillful you are. Different makers' balls bounce differently, the higher the bounce the easier it is to keep in play.

COMMUNICATING

You and your partner should work out a system of calls. Here are some of the commonly used ones:

YES - meaning play the ball because I **think** it's good

HIT - meaning play the ball because I **know** it's good

BOUNCE - meaning let the ball bounce because I **think** it's going out

NO - meaning let it bounce because I'm **sure** it's out

MINE - meaning give me room to hit this one myself

YOURS - meaning I'm expecting you to hit this one

ONE - meaning hit the ball after it comes off the first wire

TWO - meaning let the ball come off both wires before hitting

STAY - stay where you are because I'm going where you were

GO - meaning this is your shot and you are going to have to run for it

SWITCH - meaning we are going to exchange positions

COVER - meaning I'm out of position, you have to cover more court

There are some calls that should not be made. For example:

NICE GET or **GREAT SHOT** or any other comment that can be saved till the point's over

HIT IT - when the ball is on the **opponents'** side of the net and you want to talk them into something

Whatever your approach to a calling system, even if it's only YOU or HAH! or WATCH IT, don't just stand there, say **something!**

8 WAYS PADDLE IMPROVES YOUR TENNIS GAME

1. Instills confidence in playing the net because you get so many overheads and volleys to hit.
2. Speeds up your reaction time and sharpens your reflexes because it's a small-court game.
3. Disciplines your service attitude. Breaks the bad habit of belting the first, babying the second.
4. Teaches that steadiness is a better strategy than flashiness, and that you win by cutting down on errors, not hitting placements.
5. Shows you that communicating with your partner is what good teamwork is all about.
6. Brings home the importance of your return of service, the pivotal stroke in tennis doubles.
7. Proves that you must recover good court position and move without the ball between shots.
8. By providing variety, the spice of life, helps keep you from becoming stale or over-tennised.

100 WIRE SHOTS IN 2 MINUTES!

Get a ball. Stand facing the corner and rally with yourself. Take the ball whichever way it comes off the wires and play it on one bounce. This drill will improve your lateral movement while it trains your personal radar system. Two minutes of this kind of self-programming will have you winded but wise in the ways of the wires.

(ZONING)

WHEN THE BALL HAS BEEN HIT HERE:

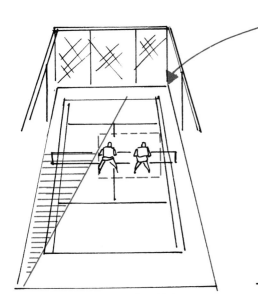

CORRECT PLAY: Both of you move laterally with the ball and give away the wing.

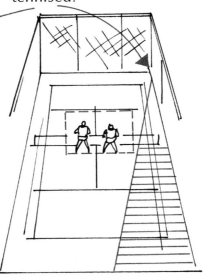

CARELESS PLAY: If you both stay put, you leave the alley open for a passing shot.

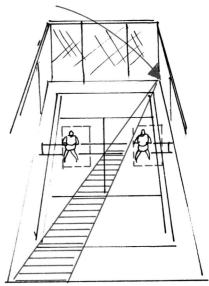

CARELESS PLAY: If only one player zones, you leave the middle open for a drive.

111

GLOSSARY

A

ace - a serve that is untouched by the receiver
ad - short for advantage; the point after deuce
ad in - alternate form of advantage server
ad out - alternate form of advantage receiver
angle volley - a shot aimed low into the side screen, hit at an acute angle to the net
approach volley - first volley; the shot hit by the server as he takes the net

B

backcourt - the area between the baseline and the service line
backhand court - popular but incorrect term for the left court
backspin - see SPIN
backswing - the act of taking the paddle back behind the body in preparation for the stroke itself
bad caller - a player who habitually calls the close ones in his own favor

block - a return accomplished with no backswing and little or no followthrough
blitz - charging to the net behind a return of service attempting to steal the offensive
box - slang for the service area
break - as in service break, a game lost by the serving team

C

carry - an illegal maneuver in which the ball is held on the paddle briefly and slung back rather than hit cleanly. See DOUBLE HIT
chip - a short, angled return with backspin
closed - descriptive of the paddle face, the body stance or the style of grip. A closed face is pitched forward; a closed stance means the shoulders are turned away from the net; a closed grip is the Eastern Forehand
corner - either the corner of the court itself or the corner where the wires are at right angles
cover - (1) to cover the ball means rolling the paddle upward and pronating the arm to achieve topspin (2) to cover for one's partner means to adjust court poisition so as not to leave too wide an opening
crosscourt - a shot hit diagonally over the net

D

deck - the entire playing surface including court and out-of-bounds area
deep - (1) in the backcourt (2) alternative for a call of ''out'' or ''long''
deuce - see SCORING
dink - a soft, dipping, angle shot, usually a service return
double fault - common but incorrect term for service fault, a carryover from tennis
double hit - an illegal maneuver in which the ball makes two separate contacts with the paddle on the same stroke. The CARRY is a smooth version of a double hit.
doubles - two players vs. two players
down the line - a shot that is more or less parallel to and near the sideline or alley line; sometimes called up the line
drive volley - a hard hit volley with an extended backswing and followthrough
drop shot - common but incorrect term for a drop volley; a true drop shot is a groundstroke
drop volley - a touch shot that clears the net and drops close to it

E

elbow - (1) ''the elbow'' is a synonym for tensing up in a match (2) tennis elbow is a medical trauma, lateral humeral epicondylitis, a painful inflammatory condition
error - failure to get the ball back over the net when you are reasonably expected to do so

F

face - the hitting surface of the paddle
fault - a service error
FBI - abbreviation of First Ball In, an alternative to First One In
fifteen - see SCORING
first one in - an informal and extralegal announcement by the server that he is going to be practicing until one of his serves goes in, at which point play automatically starts
first volley - see APPROACH VOLLEY
flag - flagging the ball means volleying a ball that would otherwise have gone out
flat - having no spin
flocking - the fuzz on the ball
footfault - a service fault by reason of improper position or action
forced error - inability to return the ball because the opponent's shot was too pressing, although not quite an outright winner
forehand court - popular but incorrect term for the right court
forty - see SCORING

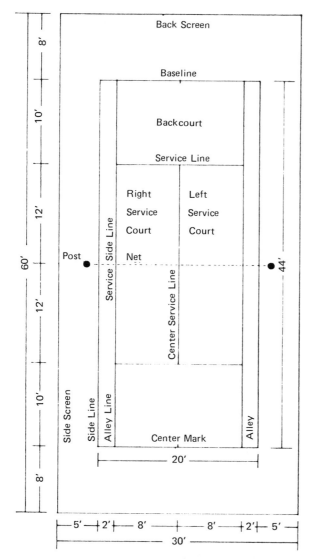

112

G

get - slang for a retrieve, as in "good get"
grip - (1) the method of holding the paddle, e.g. Continental Grip (2) the handle of the paddle itself (3) the wrap on the handle of the paddle
grooved - a grooved stroke is a well-trained stroke hit the same way every time, without conscious awareness of the mechanics, i.e. automatically well done
groundstroke - any stroke hit after the ball bounces on the deck, as differentiated from volleys and serves

H

half volley - not a volley, actually, but a groundstroke hit just after the bounce

K

kicker - a high-bouncing, angled ball that spins away from or into the receiver, accomplished usually by hitting with twist

L

let - a point to be replayed
let cord - common but incorrect term for a net cord shot

M

mixed doubles - a man and a woman vs. a man and a woman

N

net - the interlaced cord that forms the divider between halves of the court. The term should not be used interchangeably with screen or wire.
net cord shot - a ball that just ticks the top of the net cord; also a ball that rolls along the top of the net cord and then drops into the court
nick - slang term for the corner where the wires are at right angles
not up - not hitting the ball until it has bounced a second time

O

one - (1) a call to partner suggesting that the ball be played off the first wire and not be permitted to hit the second wire (2) as in "stay for one" or "change for one" referring to the first game of the set about to be played
open - descriptive of the paddle face, the body stance or the style of grip. An open face is pitched backward; an open stance means the shoulders are more or less parallel to the net; an open grip is the Continental
out - (1) a call to inform the opponents that their shot did not land within the court (2) an informal call to partner (while the ball is still in the air) that the ball is probably going out (3) indicating the receiving team, as in "ad out" (4) freely, without restraint, as in "hit out"
overhand - an incorrect term for overhead
overspin - see SPIN

P

passing shot - a drive or lob that gets past the net player
percentages - percentage play is the strategy of consistently hitting the shot that the situation calls for; a poor percentage shot is one that risks the point
pitch - synonym for tilt of the paddle face
play a let - agreement to replay the point
poach - intercept a ball that would normally be hit by your partner, especially a return of service

R

rally - the act of hitting the ball back and forth over the net
ready position - weight forward, knees bent, paddle head up, body low, completely alert in expectation of playing the ball

receiver - the player who is being served to
return of service - the first shot hit by the receiver; it must be either a groundstrroke or a screenshot

S

screens - the vertical playing surface of the superstructure, usually 1'' hexagonal mesh chicken wire. Balls played off the screens may be called screen shots, screenplay, wire shots, wires, etc. Incorrectly called the net or the wall by some players.
scoring - the progression is: love, fifteen, thirty, forty, game. If both teams have forty it is called deuce. The next point is ad. The team that wins 6 games, by a 2 game margin or better, wins the set. If both teams win 6 games a tiebreaker is played.
set point - needing only one more point to finish the set
short hop - hitting a ball on the short hop means close to the deck, just after it has bounced
slap - a shot that is more a poke than a stroke; slapping means not following through, not stroking smoothly
slice - see SPIN
smash - a hard-hit overhead
snow gates - the rectangular gates around the deck that open to permit snow removal; also called snow boards
spin - rotation of the ball; varieties of spin include topspin (also called top and overspin), slice (which means sidespin on some shots and backspin on others), underspin (also called backspin), and twist (a combination of top and sidespin). Reverse sidespin, chop, and chip are other terms used to describe varieties of spin. A chop, for example, is severe underspin. The way a ball spins depends on the angle of the paddle face at contact and the movement of the paddle through the swing.
spinning the paddle - the usual way of determining which team will serve first
strategy - the overall plan of play, e.g. playing the woman in mixed doubles. See TACTICS
stroke - a specific shot. The strokes are: serve (or service), volley, overhead, forehand, backhand, lob, half volley. Return of service, wires, dinks, etc., are shots but not strokes per se. Stroke as a verb means to hit the ball.
superstructure - the uprights, screens, lights, doors and snow gates as a whole

T

tactics - the method of carrying out the strategy, e.g. blitzing on the woman's serve, driving at her body, working her over in the wires
thirty - see SCORING
tiebreaker - a playoff when the score is 6 games all. The winner of the tiebreaker wins the set 7-6
top, topspin - see SPIN
touch - a talent for making the ball behave as if it were being stroked with the hand instead of the paddle; finesse, delicacy
twist - a sophisticated style of serving with a combination of spins; see SPIN
two - a call to partner suggesting that the ball be played off the second wire

W

warm up - the practice period before starting to play for points
wide - out; beyond the sideline
winner - a shot that wins the point outright
wires - synonym for screens

Z

zoning - moving laterally with the ball to close off the most vulnerable areas of the court

113

It is something of a coincidence that so many of the words that describe the nature of the game of paddle begin with the letter P. With a minimum of elucidation, here are some of them.

Patience. It's a virtue.

Partnership. Once you have found him/her never let go.

Position. There's a right place to be for every shot.

Pace. Yes, on the forehand drive. No, on the overhead.

Placement. Ball control is the key to winning.

Preparation. Get your paddle back sooner.

Purpose. What you should hit every ball with.

Parallel. Both players up or both back.

Practice. Definitely worth the investment in time.